WELCOME!

On behalf of Splash! Publications, we would like to welcome you to *California History*, one of several books in our State History series. Since this curriculum was designed by teachers, we are positive that you will find it to be the most comprehensive program you have ever utilized to teach students about California's history. We would like to take a few moments to familiarize you with the program.

THE FORMAT

California History is a seven lesson program. Our goal is a curriculum that you can use the very first day you purchase our materials. No lessons to plan, comprehension questions to write, activities to create, or vocabulary words to define. Simply open the book and start teaching.

Each of the seven lessons requires students to complete vocabulary cards, read about a history topic, and complete a Reading comprehension activity that will expose them to various standardized test formats. In addition, each lesson includes a balanced mix of lower and higher level activities for students to complete. Vocabulary quizzes; thought provoking discussion questions; mapping activities utilizing number coordinates; time lines; following written directions activities; writing and journaling activities that utilize graphic organizers; and grid math are the types of activities that will guide students on their journey through *California History*.

THE LESSON PLANS

On the next several pages, you will find the Lesson Plans for *California History*. The Lesson Plans clearly outline what students must do before, during, and after each lesson. Page numbers are listed so that you will immediately know what you need to make copies of before beginning each lesson. The answers to all activities, quizzes, and comprehension questions can be found on pages 86-92.

THE VOCABULARY

Each lesson features words in bold type. We have included a Glossary on pages 81-85 to help students pronounce and define the words. Unlike a dictionary, the definitions in the Glossary are concise and written in context. Remember, we're teachers! Students will be exposed to these vocabulary words in the comprehension activities. They will also be tested on the vocabulary words four times throughout their study of *California History*.

Students will be responsible for filling out and studying the vocabulary cards. You may want to have students bring in a small box for storing their vocabulary cards. We don't have to tell you that incorporating these words into your Reading and Spelling programs will save time and make the words more meaningful for students.

CALIFORNIA'S SOCIAL STUDIES STANDARDS

California History was designed to align with the California State Standards for Social Studies. These standards serve as a framework for California Social Studies curricula by providing student performance expectations in the areas of History and Social Sciences. On pages xiii-xiv, you will find quick reference charts listing the History and Social Sciences standards and the lessons and activities in *California History* that correlate with these standards.

CORE STANDARDS: THE "BIG IDEAS"

Core Standards help teachers prioritize instruction and connect the "big ideas" students need to know in order to advance. California is one of several states incorporating the Common Core Standards into its Learning Standards. As a reading-based program, *California History* fosters literacy in Social Studies.

At the same time that students are learning important factual content about the history of California, they are meeting the Common Core Standards for English Language Arts by referring to details and examples in the text to answer questions and draw inferences, participating in thought-provoking discussions, creating, utilizing, and interpreting maps and other graphics for a deeper understanding of the text, constructing time lines for themselves and California's famous explorers, writing imaginative stories and letters about their adventures in the Mexican War, and conducting a research project about the California Territory in order to make connections to the "big ideas" of California's history. Alignment to the Common Core Standards has been noted in the Lesson Plans.

THE COPYRIGHT

Revised Edition, 2013

Text Copyright © 2009 by SPLASH! Publications, Glendale Arizona

Illustration Copyright © 2009 by SPLASH! Publications, Glendale Arizona

Illustrations and cover design by Victoria J. Smith

ISBN 978-1-935255-12-3

OUR OTHER TITLES

COMPLETE STATE HISTORY PROGRAMS

Do American History!
Do Arizona!
Do California!
Do Colorado!
Do Florida!
Do Nevada!
Do New Mexico!
Do Texas!
Do Washington!

LITERATURE STUDY GUIDES

Charlotte's Web
Cricket in Times Square
Enormous Egg
Sarah, Plain and Tall

AMERICAN HISTORY SERIES

New World Explorers
Spanish Explorers & Conquistadors
The Thirteen Original Colonies
Early American Government
The American Revolution
Slavery in America
Westward Expansion
The Civil War
World War I

U.S. REGION SERIES

The Middle Atlantic States
The New England States
The Great Lakes States
The Great Plains States
The Southeast States
The Southwest States
The Mountain States
The Pacific States

STATE HISTORY SERIES

Arizona Geography
Arizona Animals
Arizona History
Arizona Government & Economy
California Geography
California Animals
California Government & Economy
Florida Geography
Florida Animals
Florida History
Florida Government & Economy
Illinois History
Indiana History
Michigan History
Ohio History
Texas Geography
Texas Animals
Texas History
Texas Government & Economy

PRIMARY SERIES

Leveled Math: Addition Bk 1
Leveled Math: Addition Bk 2
Leveled Math: Subtraction Bk 1
Leveled Math: Subtraction Bk 2
National Holidays
National Symbols
Poems for Every Holiday
Poems for Every Season

COMMON CORE LANGUAGE UNITS

First Grade Common Core Language
Second Grade Common Core Language
Third Grade Common Core Language
Fourth Grade Common Core Language

TABLE OF CONTENTS

CALIFORNIA HISTORY

TABLE OF CONTENTS

CALIFORNIA HISTORY (CONTINUED)

Lessons at a Glance

1. Before reading California's First People, students will:
- complete Vocabulary Cards for *abalone, abandoned, archaeologists, Asia, burrows, centuries, ceremonies, channel, climate, coast, continent, culture, descendants, dwellings, hearth, inhabited, intruders, North America, recreational, resources, submerged, temporary, tule. (pg. 1)*

After reading California's First People *(pps. 2-7)*, students will:
- answer California's First People Reading Comprehension Questions. *(pg. 8)*
- use number/letter pairs to plot dwellings of California's Early Cultures on a map. *(pps. 9-11)*
- take a Vocabulary Quiz for California History Part I. *(pps. 12-13)*

CALIFORNIA'S FIRST PEOPLE LESSON COVERS THESE 4TH GRADE CORE STANDARDS:
CC.4.RI.1, CC.4.RI.4, CC.4.RI.7, CC.4.RI.10, CC.4.RF.3A, CC.4.RF.4A, CC.4.RF.4C, CC.4.L.4A, CC.4.L.4C, CC.4.L.6

COMMON CORE STRAND CODE:
CC = COMMON CORE
RL = READING-LITERATURE
RI = READING INFORMATIONAL TEXT
RF = READING FOUNDATIONS SKILLS
W = WRITING
SL = SPEAKING LISTENING
L = LANGUAGE

Lessons at a Glance

2. Before reading California's Explorers, students will:
- complete Vocabulary Cards for *agriculture, anchored, attaining, autobiography, biographies, blockade, canals, capital, captive, cargo, conquered, convinced, currents, defeating, emperor, empire, expand, fertilized, historians, hoax, irrigate, knight, ransom, recruit, sacrificed, sculptures, shallow, voyage.* *(pg. 1)*

After reading California's Explorers *(pps. 14-18)*, students will:
- answer California's Explorers Reading Comprehension Questions. *(pg. 19)*
- differentiate between primary and secondary sources. *(pg. 20)*
- create a time line for Spanish explorers in Time Travel Part I. *(pg. 21)*
- create a personal time line in Time Travel Part II. *(pg. 22)*
- take a Vocabulary Quiz for California History Part II. *(pps. 23-24)*

CALIFORNIA'S EXPLORERS LESSON COVERS THESE 4TH GRADE CORE STANDARDS:
CC.4.RI.1, CC.4.RI.4, CC.4.RI.7, CC.4.RI.10, CC.4.RF.3A, CC.4.RF.4A, CC.4.RF.4C, CC.4.L.4A, CC.4.L.4C, CC.4.L.6

COMMON CORE STRAND CODE:
CC = COMMON CORE
RL = READING-LITERATURE
RI = READING INFORMATIONAL TEXT
RF = READING FOUNDATIONS SKILLS
W = WRITING
SL = SPEAKING LISTENING
L = LANGUAGE

Lessons at a Glance

3. Before reading Spanish Missions, students will:
- complete Vocabulary Cards for *allies, aqueducts, blacksmithing, Christianity, citizens, colonies, construction, convert, customs, epidemic, fertile, foreign, former, founded, grants, harbors, harsh, independence, industry, kidnapped, livestock, missions, orchards, priest, profitable, prosperous, quadrangle, raided, rancherias, rebel, small pox, tallow, tanning.* *(pg. 1)*

After reading Spanish Missions *(pps. 25-28)*, students will:
- answer Spanish Missions Reading Comprehension Questions. *(pg. 29)*
- complete discussion questions for Spanish Missions/Russian Explorers. *(pg. 30)*
- use number coordinates to plot California's Missions on a map. *(pps. 31-36)*
- follow written directions for drawing a Sea Otter. *(pps. 37-38)*
- take a Vocabulary Quiz for California History Part III. *(pps. 39-40)*

THE SPANISH MISSIONS LESSON COVERS THESE 4TH GRADE CORE STANDARDS:
CC.4.RI.1, CC.4.RI.4, CC.4.RI.7, CC.4.RI.10, CC.4.RF.3A, CC.4.RF.4A, CC.4.RF.4C, CC.4.SL.1A, CC.4.SL.1D, CC.4.L.4A, CC.4.L.4C, CC.4.L.6

COMMON CORE STRAND CODE:
CC = COMMON CORE
RL = READING-LITERATURE
RI = READING INFORMATIONAL TEXT
RF = READING FOUNDATIONS SKILLS
W = WRITING
SL = SPEAKING LISTENING
L = LANGUAGE

Lessons at a Glance

4. Before reading Americans in California, students will:
- complete Vocabulary Cards for *disbanded, emigration, Europe, Great Britain, incisor, mansion, Mormon, outlaw, pioneers, rodent.* *(pg. 1)*

After reading Americans in California *(pps. 41-43)*, students will:
- answer Americans in California Reading Comprehension Questions. *(pg. 44)*
- read about John Bidwell and answer thought provoking questions. *(pps. 45-46)*
- utilize a graphic organizer to write a Mountain Man Story. *(pps. 47-48)*
- follow written directions for drawing a Beaver. *(pps. 49-50)*

THE AMERICANS IN CALIFORNIA LESSON COVERS THESE 4TH GRADE CORE STANDARDS:
CC.4.RI.1, CC.4.RI.4, CC.4.RI.7, CC.4.RI.10, CC.4.RF.3A, CC.4.RF.4A, CC.4.RF.4C, CC.4.W.2A, CC.4.W.2B, CC.4.W.2C, CC.4.W.2D, CC.4.W.4, CC.4.W.5, CC.4.W.8, CC.4.W.10, CC.4.L.2A, CC.4.L.2B, CC.4.L.2C, CC.4.L.2D, CC.4.L.4A, CC.4.L.4C, CC.4.L.6

COMMON CORE STRAND CODE:
CC = COMMON CORE
RL = READING-LITERATURE
RI = READING INFORMATIONAL TEXT
RF = READING FOUNDATIONS SKILLS
W = WRITING
SL = SPEAKING LISTENING
L = LANGUAGE

Lessons at a Glance

5. Before reading The Mexican War, students will:
- complete Vocabulary Cards for *boundaries, dispute, republic, superior, treaty.* *(pg. 1)*

After reading The Mexican War *(pps. 51-52)*, students will:
- answer The Mexican War Reading Comprehension Questions. *(pg. 53)*
- utilize a graphic organizer to write a Mexican War Letter. *(pps. 54-57)*

THE MEXICAN WAR LESSON COVERS THESE 4TH GRADE CORE STANDARDS:
CC.4.RI.1, CC.4.RI.4, CC.4.RI.7, CC.4.RI.10, CC.4.RF.3A, CC.4.RF.4A, CC.4.RF.4C, CC.4.W.1A, CC.4.W.1B, CC.4.W.1C, CC.4.W.1D, CC.4.W.4, CC.4.W.5, CC.4.W.8, CC.4.SL.4, CC.4.L.2A, CC.4.L.2B, CC.4.L.2C, CC.4.L.2D, CC.4.L.3A, CC.4.L.3B, CC.4.L.3C, CC.4.L.4A, CC.4.L.4C, CC.4.L.6

COMMON CORE STRAND CODE:
CC = COMMON CORE
RL = READING-LITERATURE
RI = READING INFORMATIONAL TEXT
RF = READING FOUNDATIONS SKILLS
W = WRITING
SL = SPEAKING LISTENING
L = LANGUAGE

Lessons at a Glance

6. Before reading Territorial Days, students will:
- complete Vocabulary Cards for *carpenter, enforcement, prospectors, shafts, tributaries.* *(pg. 1)*

After reading Territorial Days *(pps. 58-60)*, students will:
- answer Territorial Days Reading Comprehension Questions. *(pg. 61)*
- choose from several illustrated events to complete a Santa Fe Trail Journal. *(pps. 62-67)*

Note: You will need to make six copies of page 64 for students.

THE TERRITORIAL DAYS LESSON COVERS THESE 4TH GRADE CORE STANDARDS:
CC.4.RI.1, CC.4.RI.4, CC.4.RI.7, CC.4.RI.10, CC.4.RF.3A, CC.4.RF.4A, CC.4.RF.4C, CC.4.W.3A, CC.4.W.3B, CC.4.W.3C, CC.4.W.3D, CC.4.W.3E, CC.4.W.4, CC.4.W.7, CC.4.W.8, CC.4.W.10, CC.4.SL.1A, CC.4.SL.1D, CC.4.L.4A, CC.4.L.4C, CC.4.L.6

COMMON CORE STRAND CODE:
CC = COMMON CORE
RL = READING-LITERATURE
RI = READING INFORMATIONAL TEXT
RF = READING FOUNDATIONS SKILLS
W = WRITING
SL = SPEAKING LISTENING
L = LANGUAGE

LESSONS AT A GLANCE

7. Before reading Statehood, students will:
- complete Vocabulary Cards for *abolish, accused, adopted, charities, compromise, Congress, constitution, delegates, denied, draft, elected, extinct, governor, illegal, invasion, jury, loyal, mammal, motto, official, outraged, plantations, prohibited.* (*pg. 1*)

After reading Statehood (*pps. 68-70*), students will:
- answer California: The 31st State Reading Comprehension Questions. (*pg. 71*)
- read about Biddy Mason and answer thought provoking questions. (*pps. 72-73*)
- follow written directions to correctly color California's state flag (*pps. 74-75*)
- use number and letter coordinates to complete Statehood Grid Math. (*pps. 76-78*)
- take a Vocabulary Quiz for California History Part IV. (*pps. 79-80*)

THE STATEHOOD LESSON COVERS THESE 4TH GRADE CORE STANDARDS:
CC.4.RI.1, CC.4.RI.4, CC.4.RI.7, CC.4.RI.10, CC.4.RF.3A, CC.4.RF.4A, CC.4.RF.4C, CC.4.SL.1A, CC.4.SL.1D, CC.4.L.4A, CC.4.L.4C, CC.4.L.6

COMMON CORE STRAND CODE:
CC = COMMON CORE
RL = READING-LITERATURE
RI = READING INFORMATIONAL TEXT
RF = READING FOUNDATIONS SKILLS
W = WRITING
SL = SPEAKING LISTENING
L = LANGUAGE

CALIFORNIA STATE STANDARDS

HISTORY

	Content Standard 4.1	Content Standard 4.2	Content Standard 4.3	Content Standard 4.4	Content Standard 4.5	OTHER CONTENT
California's First People Lesson	5	1			2	Reading
First People comprehension	5	1				Reading Language
Early Culture mapping	1, 2, 5	1				Reading Math
California's Explorers Lesson	4	2	2			Reading
Explorer comprehension	4	2	2			Reading Language
Primary and Secondary Sources		1,2,3				Reading Language
Explorer time line		2				Reading Language
Spanish Missionaries Lesson	4, 5	1, 3, 4, 5, 6, 8	2			Reading
Spanish Missionaries comprehension	4, 5	1, 3, 4, 5, 6, 8				Reading Language
Spanish and Russian discussion		1,3				Reading Language
California's Mission mapping	1, 2, 4	1, 3, 4, 5, 6				Reading Math
How to Draw a sea otter	5	3				Language Art
Americans in California Lesson	4, 5	8	1, 2	4		Reading
Americans in California comprehension	4, 5	8	1, 2	4		Reading Language
Mountain Man story	5	8	2	4		Language
How to Draw a beaver	5			4		Language Art
Famous People: John Bidwell			2			Reading
Mexican War Lesson		7				Reading Language

CALIFORNIA STATE STANDARDS

HISTORY	Content Standard 4.1	Content Standard 4.2	Content Standard 4.3	Content Standard 4.4	Content Standard 4.5	OTHER CONTENT
Mexican War comprehension		7				Reading Language
Mexican War letter		7				Reading Language
Territorial Days Lesson	4, 5		1, 2, 3	2, 4		Reading
Territorial Days comprehension	4, 5		1, 2, 3	2, 4		Reading Language
Santa Fe Trail journal	5		2, 3	4		Language Art
California's Statehood Lesson			3, 5			Reading
Statehood comprehension			5			Reading Language
Famous People: Biddy Mason			2, 4			Reading Language
Statehood grid math	1, 2					Reading Math

Vocabulary Card

word: _____

definition: _____

_____

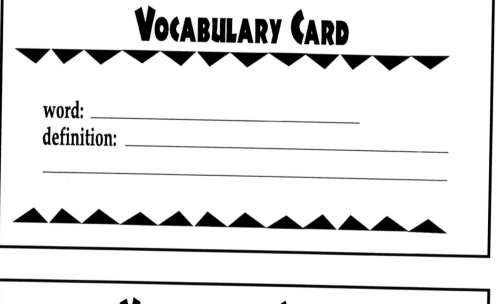

Vocabulary Card

word: _____

definition: _____

_____

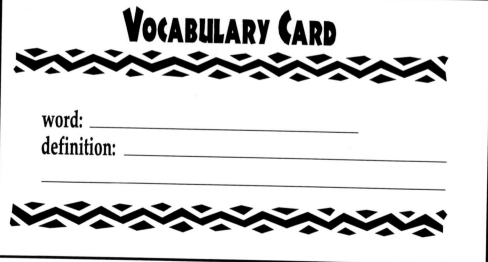

Vocabulary Card

word: _____

definition: _____

_____

CALIFORNIA'S FIRST PEOPLE

The first humans to live in **North America** and the area now known as the state of California were hunters. **Archaeologists** (ar•kee•OL•uh•jists) believe that these hunters were originally from the **continent** of **Asia**. They entered North America by walking across the Bering Land Bridge.

The Bering Land Bridge was actually a strip of frozen ice that was 1,000 miles wide. It connected northeast Asia to western Alaska thousands of years ago. Wild animals crossed back and forth over the Bering Land Bridge. The Asians followed the animals into North America. When the ice melted, the frozen bridge disappeared and the water raised the level of the sea. The people who followed the animals into North America had no way to get back to Asia. They continued following the wild animals throughout North America. Some of these people settled in California.

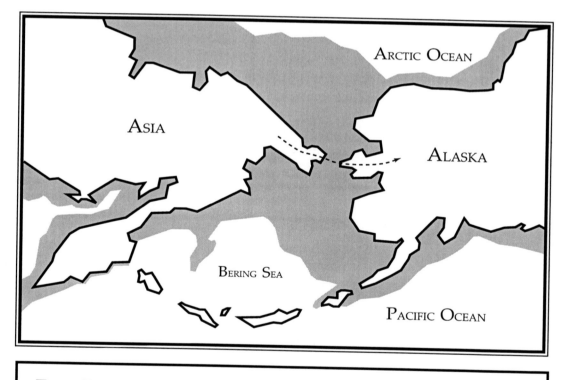

FAST FACTS

• In 1728, Russian explorer and sea captain Vitus Bering was sent to the North Pacific to find out if North America and Asia were connected by land. Vitus Bering sailed around the northeast corner of Asia, proving that there was water between Asia and North America.
• In 1741, Vitus Bering returned to the North Pacific with his crew of 10,000 men on a journey to find and make maps of the west **coast** of America.

CALIFORNIA'S EARLY NATIVE AMERICANS

California's first people arrived about 12,000 years ago from the north and the east. Over the next **centuries**, these people crossed California's steep mountains and dry deserts in search of food and shelter. We call their **descendants** Native Americans. Long before the arrival of Spanish explorers, there were about 300,000 Native Americans living in 22 separate tribes throughout California. More than 135 different languages were spoken by California's first people.

California's early tribes of Native Americans can be divided into six regions or **culture** areas. They included the Northwestern, Northeastern, Central, Great Basin, Southern, and Colorado River cultures. Each culture spoke its own language and had its own way of life. The daily lives of each culture depended upon the **climate**, plants, and animals available in each area. Tall mountain ranges and huge desert areas separated the cultures and made it difficult to travel long distances and come in contact with one another.

THE NORTHWESTERN CULTURES

The Hupa (HOO•puh), Shasta, and Yurok cultures once inhabited the northwestern corner of California. The Hupa lived in the Hoopa Valley along the Trinity River. The Shasta lived along the upper Klamath River in the northernmost part of California. The Yurok lived along the lower Klamath River on the Pacific Coast of northwestern California.

The Northwestern cultures found more than enough food in this part of California. Twice a year they fished for king salmon along the rivers of their territory. They also gathered shellfish from the ocean, plants in the forest, and acorns from the oak trees.

The Northwestern cultures made very good use of the cedar trees that grew in thick forests throughout the region. Houses big enough to hold large families and canoes strong enough to travel the ocean on fishing trips were made from cedar trees. Blankets and rugs were woven from the fiber of the cedar bark. Tools, baskets, and bowls were made from cedar trees as well.

The Northwestern cultures also made totem poles from cedar trees. Totem poles were carved with pictures of family history and showed faces of animal and human spirits that helped the Native Americans throughout their lives. They were created to mark land owned by different tribes, to honor the dead, or in celebration of important events.

TOTEM POLE

NORTHWESTERN DWELLINGS

The Northwestern cultures lived in small villages where they built houses out of cedar or oak planks. Their houses were **submerged** partly beneath the ground over a pit that ran the entire length of their **dwellings**. Each house had a fire **hearth** in the center, a small round doorway in one corner, and a porch made out of stone.

NORTHWESTERN PLANK HOUSE

The Northwestern cultures were considered wealthy because of the available **resources** in this part of California. The richest men in the Northwestern tribes were the leaders. Wealth was based upon the number of woodpecker scalps, white deerskins, and seashells that a man owned. These items were treated like money and could be used to buy other things that the tribes needed. Trade was very important to the Northwestern cultures. They often traveled as far as northern Asia to trade for iron to make knives.

THE NORTHEASTERN CULTURES

The Modoc (MOE•doc) and Achumawi (uh•KOE•muh•we) cultures lived in northeastern California. The Modoc people originally lived around the Klamath and Tule lakes. The Achumawi inhabited the area along the Pit River in the far northeastern corner of California. Both groups depended upon fish, acorns, roots, and vegetables that they grew in the river valleys. Deer was plentiful in northeastern California. Deep pits were dug to trap the deer which provided food and clothing for the Northeastern cultures.

To protect themselves from the cold winter climate in this part of California, the Northeastern cultures built their winter homes partly below the ground. More than six feet of snow often fell upon these earth covered dwellings during the coldest winter months.

During the summer, the Northeastern cultures built cone-shaped houses made of poles that they covered with mats made of **tule** reeds. The Modoc also built "sweat houses" where men could cleanse themselves by sweating every day. Sweathouses were also used for praying and other religious **ceremonies**.

THE CENTRAL CULTURES

The Central cultures included the Pomo, Maidu (MY•doo), Miwok (MEE•wahk), and Yokut people. These cultures lived along the Pacific Ocean, beside the rivers, and in the mountains of central California. Those tribes that lived near water were supplied with plenty of shellfish and salmon. Acorns from the oak trees were another important source of food for the Central cultures. The women used stones to pound dried acorns into powder. The powder was used to make cakes or boiled to make cereal. To gather their food, both the men and women of the Central cultures wove baskets that were so well made they could hold tiny seeds and even water without leaking.

The Central cultures built their villages far apart to give themselves plenty of room to hunt and gather food. Many different types of dwellings were built depending upon the resources available and the type of climate.

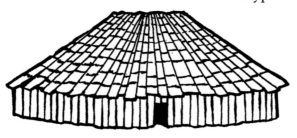

MIWOK DWELLING

The Miwok people, for example, built round dwellings covered with thick planks of bark from the forest's trees. The Pomo covered their bowl-shaped houses with three layers of plants, bark, and tule. The Maidu built dwellings that were partly below ground and covered with dirt and clay to keep out the sun's heat. The Yokut built single family dwellings that were oval-shaped and covered with tule mats. Larger houses in the Yokut villages had steep roofs and held up to ten families at the same time.

THE GREAT BASIN CULTURES

The Paiute (PIE•yoot) and Shoshone (show•SHOW•nee) peoples lived along the eastern edge of California. The land in the Great Basin contained large hills, some as much as a mile high, with low valleys in between. A dry climate in this area of California made it difficult for the Great Basin cultures to find food and water. As a result, most of their time was spent moving from one place to another in an effort to find food. This didn't leave much free time for religious ceremonies or **recreational** activities.

"First Fruits" was one important ceremony that the Great Basin cultures took time to celebrate. During the ceremony, the Native Americans gave thanks for the importance of pine nuts that they collected once a year. The men pulled pine cones from trees and the women and children piled them into large baskets that were strapped onto their backs. The pine cones were roasted until the pine nuts fell out. The pine nuts could be eaten hot or cooked further until they hardened. The hardened pine nuts were ground into pine nut flour and stored for later.

Great Basin Dwellings

Great Basin dwellings were **temporary** structures that could be easily **abandoned** when groups moved to find more food. Willow branches were put together in the shape of a cone and then covered with twigs, branches, and reeds.

During the warmer months, the Great Basin cultures depended upon ground squirrels, waterfowl, and fish. Rice grass and cattails that grew along the swampy areas of the Great Basin were ground into flour. During the fall, the Great Basin cultures collected pine nuts and hunted rabbits.

Winter was the most difficult time for the Great Basin cultures because their temporary structures offered little protection from the freezing temperatures and snow storms that blasted the Great Basin's deserts.

Food was even harder to find during the winter months because the fish were trapped beneath frozen lakes and animals hid in underground **burrows** until the cold weather was over.

During these cold winter months, women of the Great Basin cultures were busy pounding plants into shreds and weaving the fibers into clothing. They also wove baskets that were traded with other cultures for meat and animal skins.

Great Basin Dwelling

The Southern Cultures

The Southern cultures included the Chumash, Cahuilla (kuh•WE•yuh), and Serrano peoples. The Chumash inhabited the coast along the Santa Barbara **Channel** where they built villages with more than 1,000 people living in them. The Cahuilla settled in the Palm Springs area, built villages in the canyons, and enjoyed plenty of water from the nearby hot springs.

The Serrano lived in the valley between the San Gabriel and San Bernardino mountains.

The Southern cultures were hunters and gatherers who survived by making good use of the land. In addition, the Chumash fished and gathered clams, mussels, and **abalone**. They became known for making plank canoes out of redwood that were 30 feet long and could hold as many as ten people.

The Cahuilla was the only group of the Southern cultures to grow crops of corn, pumpkins, beans, squash, and melons. They dug ditches that they lined with rocks so that water from the nearby streams could flow to their small farms.

The Southern cultures lived in large villages with permanent dwellings. Throughout the year, small groups of people would leave the villages to hunt, gather plants, or trade with other Native American tribes. Although each group probably had its own design, houses in the villages were basically dome-shaped shelters made out of willow poles and covered with brush mats or strips of bark. To protect themselves from the cold weather, the Southern cultures dug a pit in the ground and built their houses over the hole. A fire in the center of the pit kept the dwelling warm. A hole was left in the top of the dwelling for the smoke to escape.

THE COLORADO RIVER CULTURES

The Colorado River cultures lived along the Colorado River in southeastern California. They included the Mohave and Yuma tribes. The Mohave inhabited the northern section of the Colorado River in California. The Yuma lived along the southern portion of the Colorado River. Extreme heat and little rain in this corner of California made life difficult for the Colorado River cultures.

The Colorado River cultures were desert farmers. They planted vegetable seeds in the river's dry bottom areas and then waited for the rain to flood the Colorado River and water their crops. Besides farming, the Colorado River tribes also gathered wild plants, hunted small animals, and fished in the Colorado River.

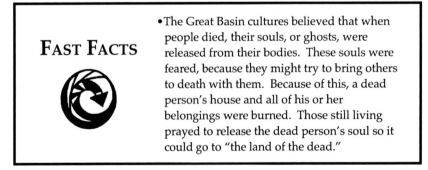

COLORADO RIVER DWELLING

The Colorado River tribes built permanent square or rectangular homes out of logs and covered them with brush mats that they wove out of weeds. They covered the brush mats with a thick layer of sand or mud to keep out the extreme heat in this part of California.

SPANISH AND ENGLISH EXPLORERS

In the 1500s, life began to change for California's Native Americans. Spanish and English explorers arrived and claimed all of the land in California for themselves. Disease, warfare, and starvation took the lives of thousands of Native Americans. By 1845, California's Native American population had been cut in half. You will soon learn about the Spanish speaking **intruders** who took control of California and forever changed the lives of California's first people.

FAST FACTS

• The Great Basin cultures believed that when people died, their souls, or ghosts, were released from their bodies. These souls were feared, because they might try to bring others to death with them. Because of this, a dead person's house and all of his or her belongings were burned. Those still living prayed to release the dead person's soul so it could go to "the land of the dead."

Name _____

❖❖❖❖❖ CALIFORNIA'S FIRST PEOPLE ❖❖❖❖❖

Directions: Read each question carefully. Darken the circle for the correct answer.

1 According to the first paragraph of California's First People, the first people in North America were –

   A Spanish explorers

   B wild animals

   C hunters from Asia

   D American soldiers

2 How did these people enter North America?

   F They swam across the Arctic Ocean.

   G They crossed the Bering Land Bridge.

   H They flew on American Airlines.

   J They traveled by boat.

3 Why did these people enter North America?

   A They were following herds of animals.

   B They were searching for freedom.

   C They wanted to live where the climate was warmer.

   D They were searching for gold and silver.

4 California's early tribes of Native Americans can be divided into six <u>cultures</u>. <u>Cultures</u> are –

   F people who live outside of their place of national birth

   G quickly moving bodies of water

   H buildings where a large amount of items are produced in the same way at the same time

   J groups of people who share a set of beliefs, goals, religious customs, attitudes, and social practices

5 Which phrase about the Northwestern cultures tells you that religion was important to them?

   A ...hunted and gathered shellfish, plants, and acorns from oak trees...

   B ...carved totem poles with faces of animal and human spirits that helped them through their lives...

   C ...considered wealthy because of the available resources in this part of California...

   D ...blankets and rugs woven from the fiber of cedar bark...

6 All of these things about the Central cultures are true <u>except</u> –

   F the Central cultures lived along the Pacific Ocean, beside the rivers, and in the mountains of central California

   G acorns were an important source of food for the Central cultures

   H the Central cultures built their villages close together for protection

   J the Central cultures wove baskets that were very well made

7 Why was survival difficult for the Colorado River cultures?

   A They were not able to find gold.

   B They often had more food than they knew what to do with.

   C The cold wet climate made it difficult for them to survive.

   D They experienced extreme heat and little rainfall in the southeast corner of California.

Answers

READING

1 Ⓐ Ⓑ Ⓒ Ⓓ   5 Ⓐ Ⓑ Ⓒ Ⓓ
2 Ⓕ Ⓖ Ⓗ Ⓙ   6 Ⓕ Ⓖ Ⓗ Ⓙ
3 Ⓐ Ⓑ Ⓒ Ⓓ   7 Ⓐ Ⓑ Ⓒ Ⓓ
4 Ⓕ Ⓖ Ⓗ Ⓙ

MAPPING: CALIFORNIA'S EARLY CULTURES

A **road atlas** is a good tool that can be used to find your way around when you are traveling away from home. A **road atlas** is a special book of maps that helps you locate cities, towns, lakes, and places of interest within a state. Numbers or letters along the bottom and sides of a **road atlas** are used as guides to help find places. These numbers and letters work together to form a kind of "grid" that puts places in an invisible box or a square. Once you know how to use the numbering and lettering system, it's easy to find your way around.

EXAMPLE:

Your family is driving through the state of California to locate where each of California's early cultures once lived. The Chumash were part of the Southern culture. They lived in large villages and built dome-shaped houses covered with brush mats. When you open your road atlas to the page that features the state of California, you see that the Chumash villages were located at E-8. Then you see a map of the entire state of California with numbers along the side of the page and letters along the bottom.

- By following the simple rule of <u>over</u> and <u>up</u>, it's easy to find the Chumash villages located at E-8 on the map. Use the letters along the bottom to slide your finger <u>over</u> to E. Then use the numbers along the side to slide your finger <u>up</u> to 8. You will find Chumash villages in this area.

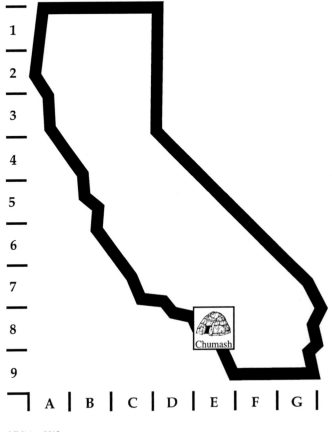

DIRECTIONS: In this activity you will create a Road Atlas for California's early cultures. As you create your Road Atlas, you will learn more about the types of dwellings built by each culture.

1. Use your scissors to carefully cut out the squares at the bottom of this page.

2. Use the blank map of California and the descriptions below to locate each of California's early cultures on your map.

3. Follow the example on the last page: If the culture is located at E - 8, use the letters along the bottom to go **over** to E. Then use the numbers along the side to go **up** to 8.

4. Glue the square containing the picture of the culture's dwelling in its correct spot on the map. Don't worry if some of the squares overlap.

5. When you have finished placing all 16 cultures, use your coloring pencils to add color to your map.

6. The Chumash culture, located at E - 8 has been placed on your map as an example.

California's Early Cultures

Achumawi	Cone-shaped dwellings covered with tule reeds	C - 1
Cahuilla	Dome-shaped dwellings covered with brush mats	F - 9
Hupa	Houses made out of cedar or oak planks	A - 2
Maidu	Dirt or clay covered dwellings	B - 3
Miwok	Round dwellings covered with thick planks of bark	C - 3
Modoc	Cone-shaped dwellings covered with tule reeds	C - 2
Mohave	Log homes covered with brush mats	G - 7
Paiute	Cone-shaped dwellings covered with twigs	D - 4
Pomo	Bowl-shaped houses made of poles, covered with thatch	B - 4
Serrano	Dome-shaped dwellings covered with brush mats	F - 8
Shasta	Houses made out of cedar or oak planks	B - 1
Shoshone	Cone-shaped dwellings covered with twigs	E - 6
Yokut	Oval-shaped dwellings covered with tule mats	C - 5
Yuma	Log homes covered with brush mats	G - 8
Yurok	Houses made out of cedar or oak planks	A - 1

Achumawi	Cahuilla	Hupa	Maidu	Miwok	Modoc	Mohave

Paiute	Pomo	Serrano	Shasta	Shoshone	Yokut	Yuma

Yurok

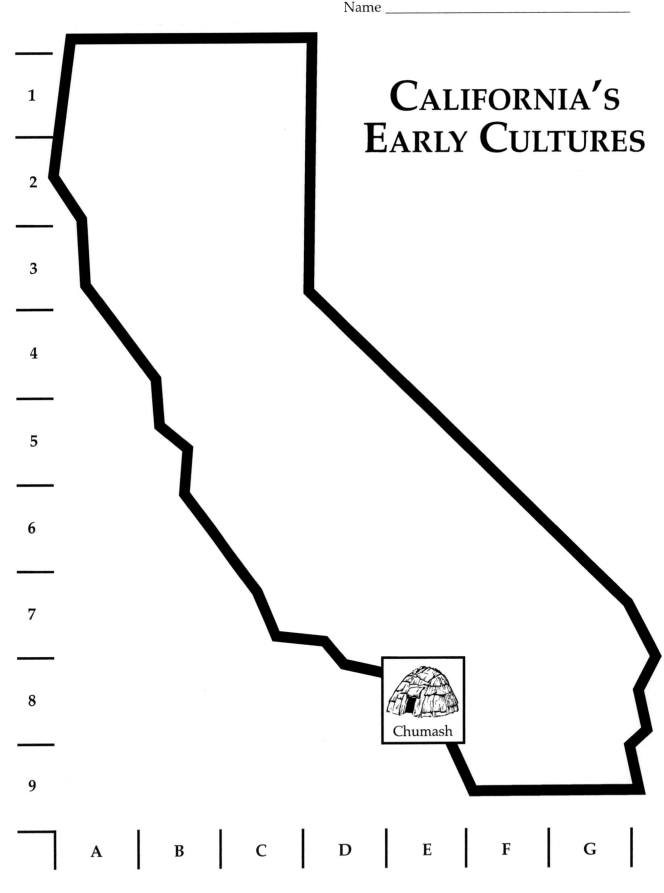

Name _____

CALIFORNIA'S EARLY CULTURES

Chumash

1
2
3
4
5
6
7
8
9

A   B   C   D   E   F   G

◈◈◈◈◈◈◈ VOCABULARY QUIZ ◈◈◈◈◈◈◈

CALIFORNIA HISTORY
PART I

Directions: Match the vocabulary word on the left with its definition on the right. Put the letter for the definition on the blank next to the vocabulary word it matches. Use each word and definition only once.

1. _____ tule

2. _____ abalone

3. _____ archaeologists

4. _____ temporary

5. _____ Asia

6. _____ submerged

7. _____ burrows

8. _____ centuries

9. _____ resources

10. _____ ceremonies

11. _____ channel

12. _____ recreational

13. _____ North America

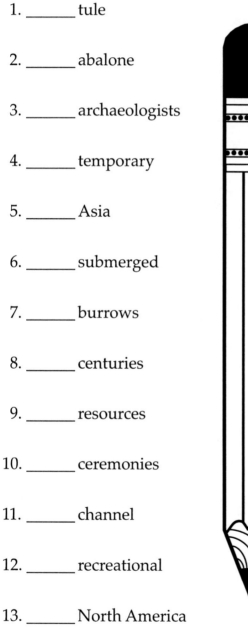

A. a large sea creature that lives in an ear-shaped shell and clings closely to rocks.

B. one of seven large areas of land on the globe.

C. partly below ground or underwater.

D. religious or spiritual gatherings.

E. periods of 100 years.

F. people who enter without permission.

G. family members who come after one has died.

H. a large plant that grows in the swampy areas of California with long flat leaves that are used for making mats and chair seats.

I. gave up completely.

J. things found in nature that are valuable to humans.

K. houses.

L. an area of land that borders water.

14. _____ intruders

15. _____ inhabited

16. _____ hearth

17. _____ dwellings

18. _____ continent

19. _____ culture

20. _____ descendants

21. _____ coast

22. _____ climate

23. _____ abandoned

M. lasting for a short period of time.

N. holes that are dug by small animals.

O. one of seven continents in the world. Bounded by Alaska on the northwest, Greenland on the northeast, Florida on the southeast, and Mexico on the southwest.

P. lived or settled in a place.

Q. the average condition of weather over a period of years.

R. scientists who study past human life by looking at prehistoric fossils and tools.

S. a group of people who share a set of beliefs, goals, religious customs, attitudes, and social practices.

T. a type of activity designed for rest and relaxation.

U. the floor of a fireplace that is covered with brick or cement and usually stretches into a room.

V. the world's largest continent with more than half of the Earth's population.

W. the deeper part of a waterway.

CALIFORNIA'S EXPLORERS

You have just finished reading about California's early Native Americans. Until the early 1500s, Native Americans were the only groups of people living in California. In fact, the only people living in all of North America were Native Americans. In the 1500s, things began to change for California's native peoples. They were visited by people they had never seen before. These strange visitors were interested in making changes in the lives of California's Native Americans. Who were these people and what did they want? To answer these questions, we must first travel back in time to the country of Mexico.

THE AZTEC EMPIRE

In the 1500s, the Aztec people lived along the Gulf of Mexico, southeast of California's Native Americans. The Aztecs were fearless warriors who created a huge **empire** that included many cities and towns. They built this empire by **defeating** other groups of people.

The Aztecs would take control of their enemy's land and make them pay yearly taxes. Warfare was considered a religious duty by the Aztecs. Prisoners taken during war were **sacrificed** to the gods.

The Aztecs designed their own calendar, built large temples for religious ceremonies, and created beautiful **sculptures**.

AZTEC FARMERS

The Aztecs were farmers who practiced slash-and-burn **agriculture**. They chopped down trees and burned a section of forest, then planted crops in the clearing. The ashes from the burned trees **fertilized** the soil. Aztec farmers also dug **canals** to **irrigate** their crops. They turned **shallow** lakes into farmland by scooping up mud from the lake bottoms to form islands. The seeds were planted in the islands and mud was added regularly to water the crops.

HERNANDO CORTÉS

In 1519, a Spanish soldier named Hernando Cortés was sent from Cuba to the Gulf of Mexico. Cortés was instructed by Cuba's rulers to explore the area known as Mexico, trade with the people found there, and bring slaves back to Cuba. He was given a few weapons, 16 horsemen, and 400 soldiers for his journey.

When his ship landed in Mexico, Hernando Cortés disobeyed the instructions of Cuba's rulers. He didn't plan to explore, trade, or take slaves back to Cuba. Instead, he decided to take control of Mexico and set up an empire for himself. Cortés was able to easily **recruit** people who had been defeated by the Aztecs and were being forced to pay yearly taxes to them. It took three months for Cortés and his large army of volunteers to travel 300 miles and reach the **capital** of the Aztec Empire.

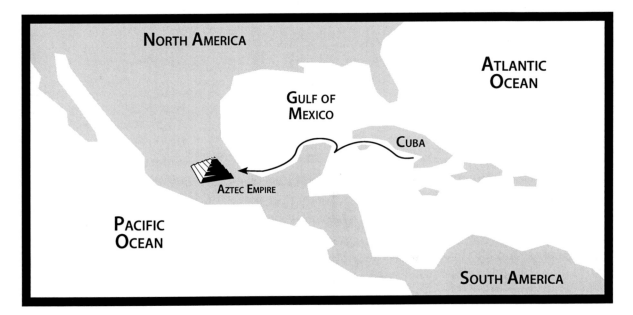

DEFEATING THE AZTECS

Hernando Cortés was greeted warmly by the Aztec **emperor**. He was given expensive gifts and even welcomed into the emperor's home. The emperor had no idea what Hernando Cortés had planned. Cortés immediately took the emperor prisoner and demanded that the Aztec's pay a **ransom** for the emperor's safe return. The Aztecs began gathering treasures to pay the ransom. Cortés's plan fell apart after the emperor was struck in the head with a rock and died.

After the death of their emperor, the Aztecs attacked Cortés and his army. Cortés fought back and formed a **blockade** around the entire city. The Aztecs were unable to get food or water. Thousands of Aztecs starved to death or died from disease. After the defeat, Cortés and his army destroyed the Aztec buildings and built Mexico City right on top of the ruins.

Hernando Cortés became a wealthy man. More importantly, he helped **expand** the Spanish empire into America by taking control of Mexico. The Spanish named their empire New Spain. In 1534, Cortés and his men traveled as far as Baja or Lower California. It wouldn't be long before the power of New Spain would be felt by the Native Americans in California and the rest of the West.

Cabeza (cah•VAY•thah) De Vaca (thay•VAH•kah)

New Spain was interested in **attaining** more wealth. From the Spanish capital in Mexico City, treasure seekers were sent out in every direction. The rulers of New Spain were eager to hear stories of land that could be **conquered** and treasures that could be found. Spanish explorer Cabeza de Vaca offered such a story.

In 1528, Spanish explorer Cabeza de Vaca and a group of about 300 men were exploring the Florida coast when a storm completely destroyed their ship. De Vaca and a small group of survivors used the wood from the wrecked ship to make rafts. A few months later, Cabeza de Vaca, an African slave, and two other Spaniards arrived half dead on the Texas coast near the present-day city of Galveston.

Cabeza De Vaca

Native Americans in Texas took the four men **captive** and used them as slaves. After several years, the four men escaped. For the next eight years, Cabeza de Vaca and his men wandered through the American Southwest on foot. In 1535, they traveled through the present-day state of New Mexico. A year later, the group reached Mexico City in New Spain.

De Vaca and his men told wild stories about their adventures. They **convinced** the Spanish rulers and other Spanish explorers that there were Seven Cities of Gold located in present-day New Mexico. According to De Vaca, even the streets in this city were paved with gold.

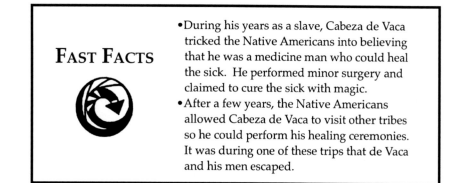

Fast Facts

- During his years as a slave, Cabeza de Vaca tricked the Native Americans into believing that he was a medicine man who could heal the sick. He performed minor surgery and claimed to cure the sick with magic.
- After a few years, the Native Americans allowed Cabeza de Vaca to visit other tribes so he could perform his healing ceremonies. It was during one of these trips that de Vaca and his men escaped.

Juan Cabrillo (cah•BREE•yo)

     In 1542, Juan Cabrillo, a Spanish explorer who had helped Hernando Cortés defeat the Aztec Empire, was sent to explore the California coast. Cabrillo hoped to find the Seven Cities of Gold and the golden paved streets that Cabeza de Vaca had described. Cabrillo also wanted to find a water route that connected the Atlantic and Pacific oceans together.

     Juan Cabrillo found neither of these things. The Seven Cities of Gold turned out to be a **hoax**. The seven cities were actually seven villages of the Zuñi people. Not one ounce of gold was ever found. Cabrillo was not able to find a water route connecting the Atlantic and Pacific oceans together because such a route did not exist. The Atlantic and Pacific oceans have always been separated by land.

     Juan Cabrillo did become the first explorer to discover the San Diego Bay and the city of Santa Barbara. He claimed the area for Spain and spent the next three months sailing northward and exploring the coast line of California. Cabrillo visited many islands along the coast including Santa Cruz, Santa Catalina, and San Clemente. Some **historians** believe that he may have sailed as far north as Oregon. Bad weather forced Cabrillo and his men to return to the San Diego Bay where they spent the winter on an area of land that Cabrillo named San Miguel (mih•GEL) Island.

     Juan Cabrillo died suddenly on January 3, 1543. Many historians believe that he died from an infection after breaking his arm.

JUAN CABRILLO

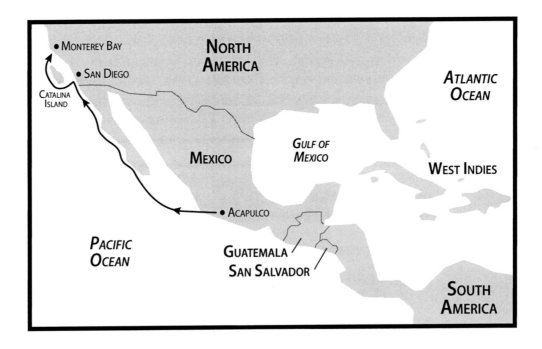

SIR FRANCIS DRAKE

In 1577, English explorer Sir Francis Drake set out on a **voyage** that would take him around the world in three years. In 1579, Drake's ship sailed along the California coast, just outside of present-day San Francisco. He **anchored** his ship and claimed the area for England's Queen Elizabeth I.

SEBASTÍAN VIZCAÍNO

In 1602, Spanish sea captain Sebastián Vizcaíno (vih•ZAH•no) entered California and explored the California coast around Monterey. The explorations of Drake and Vizcaíno did not lead to permanent settlements in California.

NO PERMANENT SETTLEMENTS

More than 200 years after Juan Cabrillo and Sir Francis Drake claimed California for their countries, there were still no permanent settlements built in California.

Building permanent settlements was the most important part of claiming new land. Permanent settlements would bring settlers to defend a country's territory against others who might want to take it away.

Fierce winds and strong ocean **currents** made it difficult for explorers to land their ships along California's coast. Many people felt that a settlement in this location would be cut off from the rest of the world. Baja California was as far north as Spanish ship captains dared to travel. As a result, California remained unsettled and in danger of being claimed by another country.

SIR FRANCIS DRAKE

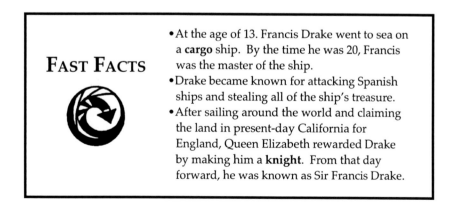

FAST FACTS

- At the age of 13. Francis Drake went to sea on a **cargo** ship. By the time he was 20, Francis was the master of the ship.
- Drake became known for attacking Spanish ships and stealing all of the ship's treasure.
- After sailing around the world and claiming the land in present-day California for England, Queen Elizabeth rewarded Drake by making him a **knight**. From that day forward, he was known as Sir Francis Drake.

◈◈◈◈◈ CALIFORNIA'S EXPLORERS ◈◈◈◈◈

Directions: Read each question carefully. Darken the circle for the correct answer.

---

1 After reading about the Aztec Empire, you learn that all of these things were true <u>except</u> –

  A they created their own calendar

  B they created huge sculptures

  C they were kind to their enemies

  D they built large temples

2 How did Aztec farmers water their crops?

  F They prayed for rain.

  G They carried water from the Gulf of Mexico in large buckets.

  H They turned on the hoses in their backyards.

  J They dug canals.

3 What can you learn by studying the map of Hernando Cortés's journey from Cuba to Mexico City?

  A He traveled east of Cuba to reach Mexico City.

  B Mexico City is west of the Pacific Ocean.

  C He traveled west of Cuba to reach Mexico City.

  D The Gulf of Mexico is in South America.

4 After reading about Hernando Cortés, you get the idea that –

  F he always did whatever his rulers told him to do

  G he was very concerned about his own success and wealth

  H he could be easily trusted

  J the defeat of the Aztec Empire left him a poor man

5 Which statement about Cabeza de Vaca is <u>true</u>?

  A He pretended to be a medicine man so he could escape slavery.

  B He never saw any Native Americans on his journey.

  C He traveled through the American Southwest alone.

  D He didn't think there was any treasure to be found in America.

6 The explorers who visited California should have strengthened their claim by –

  F trading with the Native Americans

  G making maps of the area

  H putting their country's flag in the ground

  J establishing permanent settlements

7 Why weren't explorers able to land their ships along California's coast?

  A They were too afraid of the Native Americans to land along California's coast.

  B Wild animals along the California coast made landing ships impossible.

  C Strong ocean currents and fierce winds made it difficult to land ships.

  D There were too many permanent settlements along the coast and explorers couldn't find a place to land their ships.

READING

Answers

1 Ⓐ Ⓑ Ⓒ Ⓓ	5 Ⓐ Ⓑ Ⓒ Ⓓ
2 Ⓕ Ⓖ Ⓗ Ⓙ	6 Ⓕ Ⓖ Ⓗ Ⓙ
3 Ⓐ Ⓑ Ⓒ Ⓓ	7 Ⓐ Ⓑ Ⓒ Ⓓ
4 Ⓕ Ⓖ Ⓗ Ⓙ	

the source

Think about the ways we learn about history. Reading books, seeing movies, looking at photographs, studying maps, searching the Internet, digging for bones, and holding pieces of pottery are some of the ways that we learn about the past.

There are two types of sources to help us learn about what happened in the past. Primary sources are recorded by people who were there at the time. If you have ever read a diary or an **autobiography**, then you were reading something that was written by the person who was actually recording the events and experiences as they were happening. Diaries and autobiographies are primary sources. Letters, interviews, photographs, original maps, bones, and pieces of pottery are other examples of primary sources because they give us "first-hand" knowledge of an event that took place in history.

Secondary sources are recorded by people after an event took place. Many books have been written about important historical events and people. A book written in 2005 about the life of English explorer Sir Francis Drake is a secondary source because the author wasn't actually there to interview the famous explorer and can't give any "first-hand" knowledge. Movies, **biographies,** newspaper stories, and encyclopedias are other examples of secondary sources because they give us "second-hand" knowledge of events that took place in history.

You have just finished studying about California's first people and the explorers who would change their lives forever.

In this activity, you will decide whether a source of information is a primary source or a secondary source. On the lines provided, put a "P" next to the primary sources and an "S" next to the secondary sources.

1. _____ A model of a Miwok dwelling on display at the library.

2. _____ The original map of the Bering Land Bridge drawn by Vitus Bering himself.

3. _____ A photograph of you standing by a totem pole taken while you were on vacation.

4. _____ The sword that Cabeza de Vaca carried while traveling through the Southwest.

5. _____ Juan Cabrillo's autobiography.

6. _____ A movie about the defeat of the Aztec Empire.

7. _____ An encyclopedia article written about Sir Francis Drake.

A time line is a tool used to list dates and events in the order that they happened. The time line below lists the dates that the first explorers came to America and then to California. Notice that many of the events are missing.

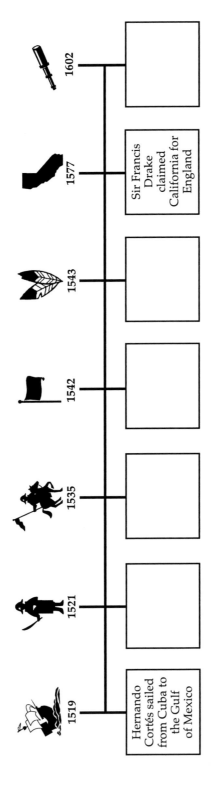

| 1519 | 1521 | 1535 | 1542 | 1543 | 1577 | 1602 |

1519 — Hernando Cortés sailed from Cuba to the Gulf of Mexico

1577 — Sir Francis Drake claimed California for England

PART I

DIRECTIONS: In the first part of this activity, you will use your information about California's Explorers to fill in the missing events on the time line. Since you were not present for any of these events, this time line would be considered a **secondary source.**

1. Use your scissors to carefully cut out each missing event. Cut along the dotted line.
2. Use your information about California's Explorers to glue the events in their proper order on the time line above.

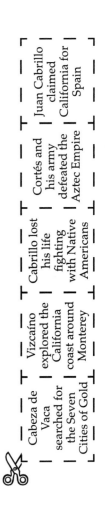

| Cabeza de Vaca searched for the Seven Cities of Gold | Vizcaíno explored the California coast around Monterey | Cabrillo lost his life fighting with Native Americans | Cortés and his army defeated the Aztec Empire | Juan Cabrillo claimed California for Spain |

PART II

DIRECTIONS: In the second part of this activity, you will create a time line of your life by listing the dates and events in order as they happened. Since you will be supplying the information about your own life, this time line would be considered a **primary source**.

1. Use the boxes drawn to make a time line of your life. Put the dates in the top boxes and the events in the bottom boxes.

2. The first date of the time line should be your birth. The last date should be the most recent event in your life.

3. Try to list only the important events. If you need more room, you may add more boxes on the back.

4. On a separate piece of paper choose one of the events from the time line and draw a picture of it.

꧁꧁꧁꧁꧁꧁꧁ VOCABULARY QUIZ ꧁꧁꧁꧁꧁꧁

CALIFORNIA HISTORY
PART II

Directions: Match the vocabulary word on the left with its definition on the right. Put the letter for the definition on the blank next to the vocabulary word it matches. Use each word and definition only once.

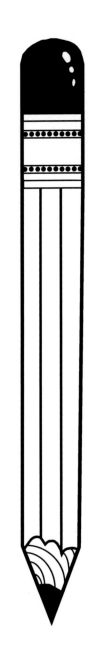

1. _____ voyage

2. _____ shallow

3. _____ sculptures

4. _____ agriculture

5. _____ anchored

6. _____ sacrificed

7. _____ recruit

8. _____ attaining

9. _____ autobiography

10. _____ ransom

11. _____ irrigate

12. _____ hoax

13. _____ historians

A. the story of your life written by you.

B. a group of territories or peoples under one ruler.

C. someone who is held without permission.

D. people who study history.

E. freight carried by a ship.

F. took over by force.

G. to find people who are willing to join a military force.

H. the male ruler of an empire.

I. journey usually made by water.

J. added a material to the soil to make crops grow better.

K. stories of a person's life written by someone else.

L. a trick.

M. man-made waterways for boats or for watering crops.

14. _____ biographies

15. _____ blockade

16. _____ canals

17. _____ fertilized

18. _____ expand

19. _____ empire

20. _____ capital

21. _____ captive

22. _____ emperor

23. _____ currents

24. _____ defeating

25. _____ conquered

26. _____ convinced

27. _____ cargo

28. _____ knight

N. the city that serves as the center of government for the state or nation.

O. killed an animal or human being as a spiritual offering.

P. planting crops and raising farm animals.

Q. talked someone into doing something your way.

R. shutting off a place to keep people and supplies from coming in or going out.

S. quickly moving bodies of water.

T. money paid for the safe return of a person who has been taken without permission.

U. a title given to a man who has done something very special for England.

V. figures or designs shaped out of clay, marble, or metal.

W. water crops by digging a ditch that leads from a body of water to a farm.

X. held a ship in place with a heavy metal object attached to a strong rope or cable.

Y. winning victory over.

Z. a hole that is not very deep.

AA. getting for oneself.

BB. grow larger.

SPANISH MISSIONS

By 1769, more than 200 years had passed since the first Spanish and English explorers had sailed their ships along California's coast. More than 300,000 Native Americans living in 22 separate tribes inhabited California before the explorers arrived. No permanent settlements had been established by Spain or England, so the Native Americans continued to live somewhat peacefully and undisturbed in California.

In 1769, Spain finally sent Catholic **priest** Father Junipero Serra to Alta or Upper California to establish California's first Spanish settlement. Father Serra **founded** the first of 21 **missions** near the city of San Diego. Father Serra had been instructed by the leaders of Spain to teach California's native peoples about the Catholic religion and prepare them for Spanish control.

The rulers in Spain wanted the Native Americans in Alta California to give up their native **customs** and become **allies** with Spain. Spain's rulers hoped that the Native Americans would help fight if Spain ever went to war against another country. Building missions along the coast and training an army of Native Americans would give Spain a firm hold on California.

FATHER SERRA'S PLAN

Father Serra and his priests were truly interested in helping California's Native Americans. They believed that teaching the Native Americans about the Catholic religion and helping them to plant crops and raise farm animals would provide them with a better way of life. Father Serra's goal was to build missions, **convert** the Native Americans to **Christianity**, and teach them how to live under Spanish control.

SPANISH PRIEST

Under Father Serra's plan, each mission would be run by the priests for ten years. After ten years, the priests would leave and the land would be given to the Native Americans who helped build the missions, plant the crops, and raise the animals. Father Serra believed that his plan would benefit the Native Americans because they would learn new methods for survival and make improvements in their land. His plan would also satisfy the Spanish rulers who wanted the Native Americans to become hard working Spanish **citizens**.

Bringing Native Americans to the Missions

In an effort to get Native Americans to come to the missions, Father Serra and his priests gave them gifts of glass beads, clothing, blankets, and food. The priests gained the trust of some of the Native Americans who agreed to move inside of the mission villages. Once they chose to live at the missions, the Native Americans were not allowed to leave without permission.

Unfortunately, most of California's Native Americans were already happy with their lives. Those groups that lived along the coast were the most **prosperous** of California's Native Americans. The Coast cultures were hunters and gatherers who enjoyed plenty of food, wealth, and open spaces. They lived in large houses made of cedar and oak. They were not eager to help Spain with its plan. Many were not willing to give up their religious customs and practice a new religion.

Native Americans who were not willing to come to the missions were **kidnapped** by Spanish soldiers. The soldiers treated the Native Americans badly, often beating them. Father Serra was very upset by the soldiers' **harsh** treatment of California's Native Americans. He asked the Spanish government to give him control over the area. Father Serra was granted control of the Native Americans, but the soldiers remained in California to keep peace at the missions. Father Serra was also given permission to build more missions.

Life at the Missions

Each of the 21 missions was built in the shape of a **quadrangle** protected by one or two gates. The largest building in each mission village was the church. Other buildings included houses, a school, farm buildings, a fort, and buildings with rooms that were used as workshops, sleeping areas, dining rooms, and kitchens. The missions were built 30 miles or about one day's journey apart from one another. Building the missions close together gave Spain greater control over California's coast.

Two priests and five or six soldiers were sent to each mission. At first, the priests wanted to teach the Native Americans in their native languages, but there were too many different languages spoken among the different tribes. Instead, the Native Americans were taught Spanish. Religion classes were taught and the Native Americans were expected to attend church services several times a day. They were not permitted to practice their native customs, speak their native languages, or celebrate their religious ceremonies. Those who tried to escape from the missions were captured and punished before being forced to return.

The Native Americans helped build the missions. The men were taught how to raise cattle and grow crops at nearby **rancherias** (ran•CHAIR•ee•uz). Other skills included leather **tanning**, wine making, **blacksmithing**, brick making, and **construction**. Women learned how to cook, sew, spin wool, and weave.

By the time the mission system ended in 1834, the Native Americans at the 21 missions had raised more than 800,000 cows, horses, hogs, sheep, and goats. They had also set up a valuable trade system with people from other countries who sailed their ships into California's **harbors**. This allowed the Native Americans to trade animal skins, **tallow**, grain, wine, olive oil, and leather goods for tools, furniture, glass, nails, cloth, and musical instruments.

DEATH FOR THE NATIVE AMERICANS

During the 65 years that Native Americans lived at the Spanish missions and rancherias, more than half of California's Native Americans died. Without knowing it, the Spanish priests, soldiers, and **foreign** traders spread **small pox** and other **epidemic** diseases throughout the mission villages. Young children and newborn babies died in large numbers. Many of the Native Americans blamed the Spanish priests because they were not permitted to perform their religious healing ceremonies.

In the early 1800s, life for the Native Americans at the missions became more difficult. The Spanish government could no longer afford to send soldiers, supplies, or money to the missions in California. As a result, the Native Americans at the missions had to work harder to produce more crops and make more items to trade. Soldiers guarded the mission gates and the Native Americans were treated like slaves. The harsh working conditions killed many of the Native Americans. The lack of freedom caused them to **rebel**. Native American women sometimes killed their own children to keep them from growing up in the missions.

RUSSIANS IN CALIFORNIA

In 1812, the first Russian explorers and traders arrived in northern California. Many of the Native Americans who lived in this region of California had been able to hide from the Spanish soldiers who kidnapped native peoples and forced them to live at the missions. Unfortunately, they were not able to escape from the Russian sailors who entered northern California from Alaska.

The Russians sailed to California for several reasons. They came to hunt sea otters for their valuable fur, grow wheat and other crops in California's **fertile** soil, and trade with the Native Americans living at the missions.

FORT ROSS

Alexander Kuskov of the American Trading Company was in charge of the first Russian settlement in northern California. He brought 25 Russian settlers and 80 native Alaskans with him. Kuskov

SEA OTTER

and his group built a settlement known as Fort Ross or Colony Ross. The location they chose for their settlement was right in the middle of the land owned by the Pomo and Miwok (MEE•wahk) people.

The Native Americans called the Russians the "undersea people." A few of the Native Americans agreed to work for the Russians. To gather more workers, the Russians **raided** Native American villages and kidnapped the women and children. The women and older children were forced to work in the fields and the Russian houses. As long as the men brought furs, meat, and fish to the Russians, the women and children were not harmed. If the Native Americans did not obey the commands of the Russians, the women and children were beaten and even killed.

THE END OF SPANISH AND RUSSIAN CONTROL

In the early 1800s, the Spanish empire began having problems. The Mexican citizens who lived in New Spain wanted freedom from the Spanish government. They were tired of being ruled by a government that was thousands of miles away. One by one, Spain's **colonies** fought for **independence**. In 1821, Mexico declared its complete independence from Spain. The Mexican government took control of New Spain and California's missions.

In 1834, the Mexican government closed the missions. The priests who lived at the missions did not think the Native Americans were ready to run the missions by themselves. The Mexican government did not listen to the priests and closed the missions anyway. Some of the land in each mission village was used for the town's buildings and farm animals. Each Native American family was given a small piece of land.

By 1841, the Russians living at Fort Ross had killed most of the sea otters along California's coast. Without the valuable sea otter furs, they could no longer continue their **profitable** fur trading business. The Russians sold Fort Ross to a man named John Sutter. The land could not be sold because it belonged to the Mexican government, but John Sutter bought all of the buildings, animals, and supplies left by the Russians. The Native Americans in northern California were free from Russian control.

THE RANCHO ECONOMY

Life for the Native Americans in California continued to be very difficult. The Mexican government gave large areas of **former** mission land to Mexican soldiers and their families as gifts for helping win the war against Spain. Mexican citizens who agreed to become Catholic and live in California for at least ten years were also given **grants** of land by the Mexican government. Raising cattle for beef and leather hides became a very profitable **industry** for California's new ranchers. It became known as the rancho economy. The rancho economy was so prosperous that it attracted the attention of the United States government who began thinking about someday making California part of the United States.

Unfortunately, the priests were gone and there was nobody to make sure that the Native Americans were treated fairly. Most of the mission land was simply taken by the Mexican government. Many Native American families gave up farming and sold their plots of land to Mexican ranchers for far less than it was worth. The money ran out quickly. With no place to live, the Native Americans found themselves hungry, homeless, and unprotected. Many wandered the streets begging for food or stole for survival. Others returned to work on the same ranches that they had just sold. The Native Americans were given food and a place to sleep, but they were not paid any money for their hard work. Life had changed forever for California's Native Americans.

FAST FACTS

- After the Mexican government took control of California, General Mariano Guadalupe Vallejo (vah•YAE•hoe) was sent to northern California to keep peace between the Native Americans and the Mexican settlers who had been granted large areas of former mission land. General Vallejo successfully removed the Native Americans from the area. For his efforts, he was given a huge land grant that included the city of Sonoma and parts of Napa and Petaluma valleys.

SPANISH MISSIONS

Directions: Read each question carefully. Darken the circle for the correct answer.

1   Who worked the farms at the Spanish missions in California?

   A   The Spanish explorers

   B   Native Americans

   C   Spanish priests

   D   Spanish children

2   After reading about Father Junipero Serra, you get the idea that –

   F   he was unkind to California's Native Americans

   G   he paid the Native Americans lots of money for their land

   H   he wasn't interested in building missions in California

   J   he was concerned about making a better life for California's Native Americans

3   Why did the Spanish government want the Native Americans to live at the missions?

   A   They knew that the Native Americans did not have homes of their own.

   B   The Native Americans were having difficulty surviving on their land in California.

   C   The Spanish rulers wanted the Native Americans to become allies with Spain.

   D   The Spanish government wanted the Native Americans to teach the Spanish children.

4   What happened to Native Americans who escaped from the missions?

   F   They were given money.

   G   They were sent to Spain.

   H   They were given land to build Native American churches.

   J   They were captured and punished before being returned to the missions.

5   The Native Americans blamed the Spanish priests for the death of their children because –

   A   the priests wouldn't let the Native Americans perform their healing ceremonies

   B   the priests let the children play outside in the cold

   C   the priests didn't want any children living at the missions

   D   the priests took all of the healthy children back to Spain

6   What can you learn from reading about Russian explorers and traders?

   F   They helped the Native Americans.

   G   They did all of the work without the help of Native Americans.

   H   They kidnapped many Native Americans and forced them to work in their fields and houses.

   J   They were kind to the Native American women and children.

7   What happened to California's Native Americans after they were released from the Spanish missions and Russian control?

   A   They became rich.

   B   They took over all the land in California.

   C   They traveled to Spain and Russia to visit their new friends.

   D   They had difficulty surviving.

Answers   READING

1   Ⓐ Ⓑ Ⓒ Ⓓ   5   Ⓐ Ⓑ Ⓒ Ⓓ

2   Ⓕ Ⓖ Ⓗ Ⓙ   6   Ⓕ Ⓖ Ⓗ Ⓙ

3   Ⓐ Ⓑ Ⓒ Ⓓ   7   Ⓐ Ⓑ Ⓒ Ⓓ

4   Ⓕ Ⓖ Ⓗ Ⓙ

Let's Talk About It

Spanish Missions and Russian Explorers

The arrival of Spanish priests and Russian explorers into California forever changed the lives of California's Native Americans. Read the questions below and write your answers on the lines provided. Attach a separate piece of paper if you need more room. Be ready to discuss some of your answers.

• **More than 300,000 Native Americans lived in California before the arrival of the Spanish priests and Russian explorers.**

If you had been a child living in a Native American village, how would you have felt about the arrival of the Spanish priests and Russian explorers? What right did your family have to keep the Spanish priests and Russian explorers from entering your village?

_____

_____

_____

If you had been a Spanish priest or the child of a Russian explorer, how would you have felt about leaving Spain or Russia to live in California? What right did you or your family have to enter the Native American villages and kidnap their families?

_____

_____

_____

• **The Spanish and Russians forced the Native Americans to work long hours in the fields and give up their Native American languages and customs.**

How do you think the Spanish and Russians were able to force the Native Americans to work in the fields and give up their languages and customs? If you had been a Native American, what could you have done to change this situation?

_____

_____

What rules and laws do we have in America that would keep this sort of thing from happening today?

_____

_____

Mapping: California's Missions

In 1769, Spain sent Catholic priest Father Junipero Serra to establish California's first Spanish settlement. Father Serra founded the first of 21 missions along California's coast. The purpose of the missions was for the Native Americans to learn about the Catholic religion and help Spain defend its claim on California.

In this activity, you will use a **grid system** to locate each of California's missions and number them according to the order in which they were founded. A **grid system** is made up of lines that come together to form squares. The squares divide a map into smaller pieces, making it easier to find important places. Learning how to use a **grid system** is easy, and will teach you an important location skill.

EXAMPLE: Mission San Diego de Alcala was founded on July 16, 1769, by Father Junipero Serra. The land for the mission was taken from the Yuma people, who were forced to live and work at the mission. The Native Americans were taught how to grow crops and bring water to their farms through a system of **aqueducts** (AH•kwuh•ducts). Mission San Diego de Alcala was located at (9,2).

To locate Mission San Diego de Alcala at (9,2), on the grid below, you would put your finger on the number 1 at the bottom of the grid, slide <u>over</u> to 9 and <u>up</u> to 2. Mission San Diego de Alcala was located in the square created when these two numbers come together. Since it was the first mission founded, the number 1 has been written in the square.

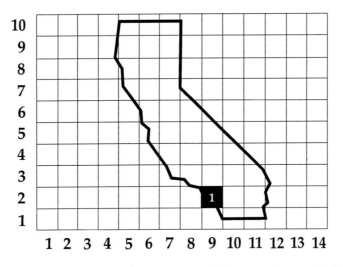

Part I

DIRECTIONS: Use the grid system and the map of California to locate California's 21 missions.

1. Follow the example above for locating each mission by going <u>over</u> and <u>up</u>. If a mission was located at (9,2), go <u>over</u> to 9 and <u>up</u> to 2.

2. When you locate a mission on the grid, write its number in the square.

3. Mission San Diego de Alcala has been placed for you as an example.

California's Missions

Mission San Carlos Borromeo de Carmelo was founded on June 3, 1770, by Father Junipero Serra. The Native Americans who lived and worked at the mission were friendly and willing to come to the mission. They helped build the mission and learned how to take care of the cattle and sheep. Mission San Carlos Borromeo de Carmelo was located at (8,16). Since it was the second mission, put the number 2 in the square.

Mission San Antonio de Padua was founded on July 14, 1771, by Father Junipero Serra. Native Americans willingly worked at the mission, raising crops of wheat and corn and vineyards of grapes. The food was eaten and traded with groups living at the other missions. Mission San Antonio de Padua was located at (10,14). Since it was the third mission, put the number 3 in the square.

Mission San Gabriel Arcangel was founded on September 8, 1771, by Father Junipero Serra. At first, the Native Americans who worked at the mission were treated poorly by the Spanish soldiers. Within time, through the kindness of the priests, the Native Americans willingly worked at the mission and helped grow large crops of corn and beans. They also made most of the soap and candles used at the rest of the missions. Mission San Gabriel Arcangel was located at (22,6). Since it was the fourth mission, put the number 4 in the square.

Mission San Luis Obispo de Tolosa was founded on September 1, 1772, by Father Junipero Serra. Native Americans from the Chumash tribe were pleased when the Spanish soldiers arrived in the area and killed the bears that were causing the Chumash people so many problems. In 1776, another group of Native Americans attacked the mission and set the tule roof on fire with flaming arrows. The Chumash tribe built a new roof out of clay bricks. Mission San Luis Obispo de Tolosa was located at (13,11). Since it was the fifth mission, put the number 5 in the square.

Mission San Francisco de Asís was founded on June 26, 1776, by Father Francisco Palóu. Since it was located in the San Francisco Bay, the mission was used to protect the bay from Spain's enemies. Unfortunately, the Spanish soldiers and priests unknowingly spread measles to the Native Americans. More than 5,000 Native Americans died from the measles. Mission San Francisco de Asís was located at (6,22). Since it was the sixth mission, put the number 6 in the square.

Mission San Juan Capistrano was founded on November 1, 1776, by Father Junipero Serra. The Native Americans were friendly from the beginning, helping to build the mission buildings and church. The Native Americans learned to spin wool, weave, sew, and carve wood. They were also skilled at making leather hides. Mission San Juan Capistrano was located at (20,5). Since it was the seventh mission, put the number 7 in the square.

Mission Santa Clara was founded on January 12, 1777, by Father Junipero Serra. By 1800, there were more than 1,200 Native Americans living at the mission. **Orchards** of fruit trees and olive trees grew well at the mission, and they had the best wheat crop of any other mission. Mission Santa Clara was located at (7,21). Since it was the eighth mission, put the number 8 in the square.

MISSION SAN BUENAVENTURA was founded on March 31, 1782, by Father Junipero Serra. This was the last mission founded by Father Serra before his death in 1784. The friendly Chumash people were happy to live at the mission which was built right in their village. The Chumash were expert boat builders. They would often travel to the Channel Islands in their 24 foot long boats to fish and gather food. They built an aqueduct which was used to bring water to their crops of vegetables, bananas, sugar cane, figs, and coconuts. Mission San Buenaventura was located at (18,8). Since it was the ninth mission, put the number 9 in the square.

MISSION SANTA BARBARA was founded on December 4, 1786, by Father Fermin Lasuen. The mission sat high on a hill overlooking the city of Santa Barbara and the Pacific Ocean. The Chumash people who lived at the mission learned to create an irrigation system that was so well built it is still used today by the city of Santa Barbara. Juana Maria, known as the "Woman of San Nicolas Island" is buried at the mission. The book *Island of the Blue Dolphins* is based on Juana Maria's life. Mission Santa Barbara was located at (15,9). Since it was the tenth mission, put the number 10 in the square.

MISSION LA PURÍSIMA CONCEPCIÓN was founded on December 8, 1787, by Father Fermin Lasuen. In 1812, an earthquake completely destroyed the church and all of the buildings at the mission. A new mission was built with walls that were four and a half feet thick in case another earthquake struck. In 1824, a group of angry Native Americans took control of the mission, only to be defeated by Spanish soldiers. The Native Americans were severely punished. Seven were put to death and 18 others were sent to prison. Mission La Purísima Concepción was located at (12,10). Since it was the eleventh mission, put the number 11 in the square.

MISSION SANTA CRUZ was founded on September 25, 1791, by Father Fermin Lasuen. Members of the Yokut tribe built and lived at the mission. The mission did well for the first few years, but in 1799, the church was completely destroyed by a rainstorm. The church was rebuilt, but in 1818, it was damaged again by Spanish settlers who lived in the nearby town. Many of the Native Americans escaped the mission and went to work in the town, leaving the mission without anyone to work in the fields or tend to the animals. Mission Santa Cruz was located at (7,19). Since it was the twelfth mission, put the number 12 in the square.

MISSION NUESTRA SENORA DE LA SOLEDAD was founded on October 9, 1791, by Father Fermin Lasuen. The word soledad means "loneliness" in Spanish. The land for the mission was actually chosen by Spanish explorers Juan Crespi and Gaspar de Portola in 1769, but there were very few Native Americans in the area, so it took 22 years to build the mission. Native Americans who lived and worked at the mission raised cattle, sheep, and horses. Mission Nuestra Senora de La Soledad was located at (11,15). Since it was the thirteenth mission, put the number 13 in the square.

MISSION SAN JOSE DE GUADALUPE was founded on June 11, 1797, by Father Fermin Lasuen. During the first year, only 33 Native Americans came to live at the mission. They were not eager to join the mission because they enjoyed their way of life. The priests offered the Native Americans gifts, and in time, Mission San Jose de Guadalupe had a large population of Native Americans living at it. Mission San Jose de Guadalupe was located at (8,21). Since it was the fourteenth mission, put the number 14 in the square.

MISSION SAN JUAN BAUTISTA was founded on June 24, 1797, by Father Fermin Lasuen. The Native Americans who lived at the mission built all of the buildings, worked in the fields, and took care of the cattle. So many Native Americans lived at the mission that the church had to be made bigger to hold 1,000 people. Mission San Juan Bautista was located at (9,20). Since it was the fifteenth mission, put the number 15 in the square.

MISSION SAN MIGUEL ARCANGEL was founded on July 25, 1797, by Father Fermin Lasuen. The Native Americans in the area had heard good things about the mission system and were eager for the priests to arrive and the mission to open. The Native Americans at the mission were excellent at making roof tiles. Between 1808 and 1809, they made 36,000 tiles that they sold or traded to other missions. Mission San Miguel Arcangel was located at (11,13). Since it was the sixteenth mission, put the number 16 in the square.

MISSION SAN FERNANDO REY DE ESPANA was founded on September 8, 1797, by Father Fermin Lasuen. The Native Americans who lived and worked at the mission learned blacksmithing, farming, ranching, carpentry, and weaving. They also became famous for their grapes and wine. There were more than 30,000 grapevines and 1,600 fruit trees planted at the mission. Mission San Fernando Rey de Espana was located at (21,7). Since it was the seventeenth mission, put the number 17 in the square.

SAN LUIS REY DE FRANCIA was founded on June 13, 1798, by Father Fermin Lasuen. This was the last mission founded by Father Lasuen before his death in 1803. The mission was known as the "King of the Missions" because it had the largest population of Native Americans. The mission village covered six acres of land and at one point there were 2,700 Native Americans living there. California's first pepper tree was planted in the mission's gardens. San Luis Rey de Francia was located at (22,4). Since it was the eighteenth mission, put the number 18 in the square.

MISSION SANTA INÉS was founded on September 17, 1804, by Father Estevan Tapis. It was located in the beautiful Santa Ynez Valley where the soil was fertile and the mission's crops and **livestock** did very well. An irrigation system built by the Native Americans brought water from the mountains several miles away. Mission Santa Inés was located at (15,10). Since it was the nineteenth mission, put the number 19 in the square.

MISSION SAN RAFAEL ARCANGEL was founded on December 14, 1817, by Father Vicente de Sarria. It was named for Saint Raphael, the angel of healing. Most of the Native Americans who came to live at the mission were very sick. The mission first served as a hospital before becoming a very successful village of Miwok people who raised more animals than any other mission in the system. Mission San Rafael Arcangel was located at (6,23). Since it was the 20th mission, put the number 20 in the square.

MISSION SAN FRANCISCO SOLANO was founded on July 4, 1823, by Father Jose Altimira. This was the last and northernmost of the 21 missions in California. It was the only mission founded after Mexico's independence from Spain and the only mission founded without first getting approval from the Catholic Church. Father Altimira was very cruel to the Native Americans who rebelled and burned all of the mission's buildings and supplies. Father Altimira was sent back to Spain and the mission was rebuilt. Mission San Francisco Solano was located at (6,24). Since it was the 21st mission, put the number 21 in the square.

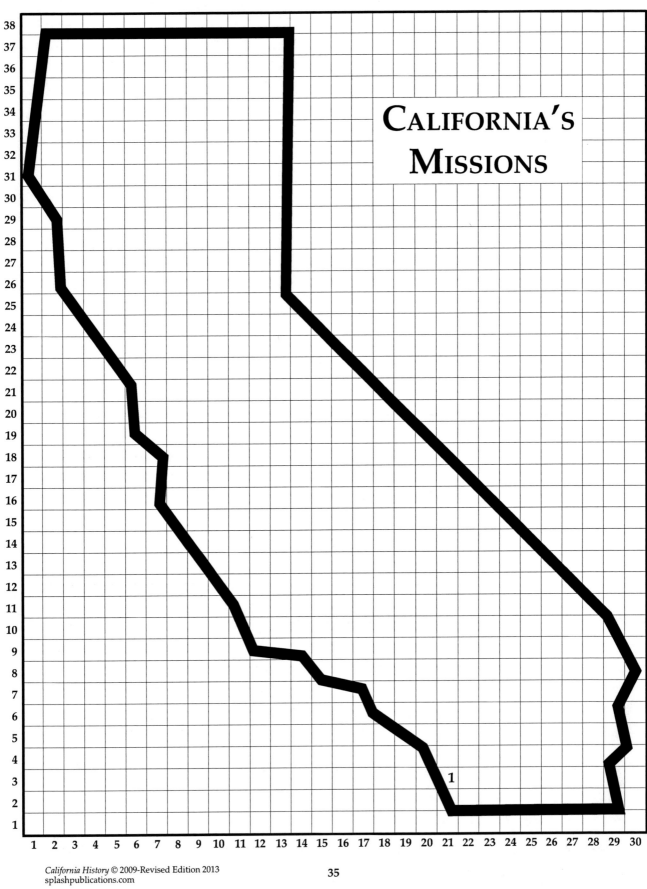

CALIFORNIA'S
MISSIONS

1

DIRECTIONS: Use the map of California's Missions to answer the questions below. Remember to answer the questions using complete sentences.

1. According to your map, in which area of California were all of the missions built?

_____

_____

_____

2. Why do you think Spain chose to build all of its missions here?

_____

_____

_____

3. Why do you think all of the missions were built so closely together?

_____

_____

_____

4. Look back at the descriptions of each mission. If you could have chosen to live at one of the missions, which one would you have chosen? Explain why.

_____

_____

_____

HOW-TO-DRAW
A SEA OTTER

Sea otters were hunted in Alaska and northern California for their fur. In the early 1800s, before the arrival of Russian hunters and fur traders, there was a large population of sea otters in the Pacific Ocean. The Russian traders forced the Native Americans to hunt the sea otters for them. By 1911, almost one million sea otters had been killed in the Pacific Ocean.

DIRECTIONS: Very lightly sketch out the first step. Then, also very lightly add step 2. Continue in this way until all four steps are completed. In each drawing, the new step is shown darker than the step before it so that the lines can be clearly seen, but you should keep your drawing very light.

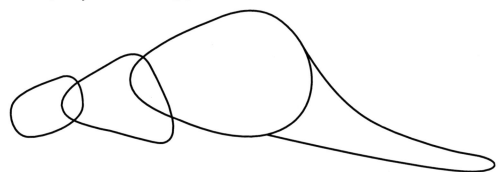

1. Draw these shapes to form the head, body and tail.

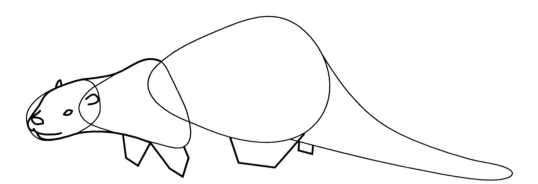

2. Add lines to form the mouth, the nose, the eye, the neck, the ears, and the legs.

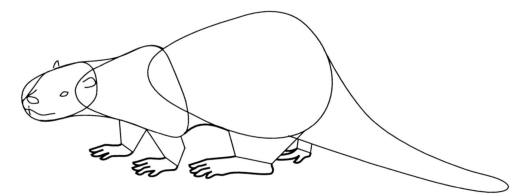

3. Add lines to form the sea otter's feet.

4. Erase guidelines, smooth out other lines and add detail

COLOR

Use your black coloring pencil to trace the outline of the nose and eye of your sea otter. Color the nose and eye black. Then use your brown coloring pencil to trace the outline of the sea otter. Color your sea otter with light and dark shades of brown.

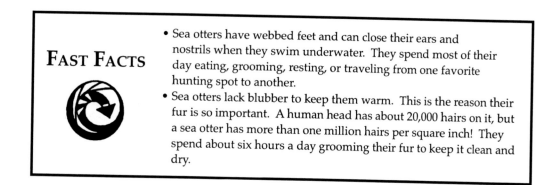

FAST FACTS

- Sea otters have webbed feet and can close their ears and nostrils when they swim underwater. They spend most of their day eating, grooming, resting, or traveling from one favorite hunting spot to another.
- Sea otters lack blubber to keep them warm. This is the reason their fur is so important. A human head has about 20,000 hairs on it, but a sea otter has more than one million hairs per square inch! They spend about six hours a day grooming their fur to keep it clean and dry.

◈◈◈◈◈◈ Vocabulary Quiz ◈◈◈◈◈◈
California History
Part III

Directions: Match the vocabulary word on the left with its definition on the right. Put the letter for the definition on the blank next to the vocabulary word it matches. Use each word and definition only once.

1. _____ tanning

2. _____ allies

3. _____ tallow

4. _____ aqueducts

5. _____ small pox

6. _____ construction

7. _____ rebel

8. _____ blacksmithing

9. _____ rancherias

10. _____ Christianity

11. _____ raided

12. _____ citizens

13. _____ quadrangle

14. _____ colonies

15. _____ prosperous

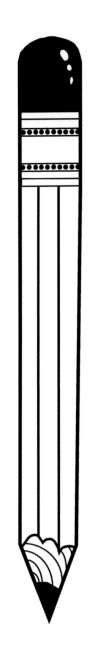

A. from another country.

B. person with the authority to perform religious ceremonies.

C. strict and sometimes unfair treatment.

D. a religion based on the life and teachings of Jesus Christ.

E. types of churches.

F. groups of people who are ruled by another country.

G. having success or wealth.

H. not under the control or rule of another.

I. small villages of Native American settlements.

J. groups of fruit trees.

K. groups of people who come together to help one another in times of trouble.

L. a type of business that makes more money than it spends.

M. people in a city, town, state, or country who enjoy the freedom to vote and participate in government decisions.

N. pipes that take water from one place to another.

16. _____ convert

17. _____ profitable

18. _____ customs

19. _____ priest

20. _____ epidemic

21. _____ orchards

22. _____ fertile

23. _____ missions

24. _____ foreign

25. _____ livestock

26. _____ kidnapped

27. _____ former

28. _____ industry

29. _____ founded

30. _____ grants

31. _____ harbors

32. _____ harsh

33. _____ independence

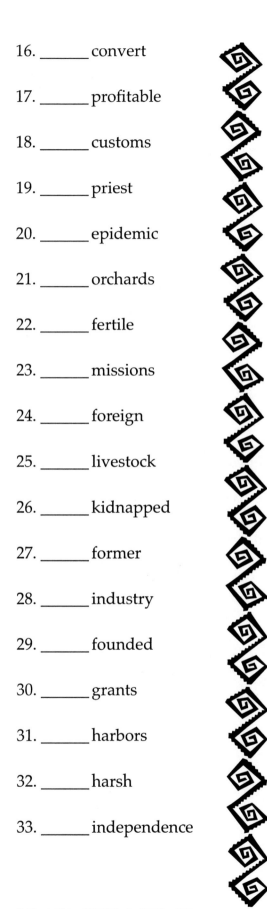

O.   sheltered parts of water deep enough to provide ships a place to anchor.

P.   usual ways of doing things.

Q.   a rectangular area surrounded on all sides by buildings.

R.   coming from the past.

S.   animals raised on a farm to eat or sell for profit.

T.   gifts of land.

U.   a white solid fat produced by heating the fatty tissues of cattle and sheep and used for making candles and soap.

V.   work that involves putting something together.

W.   disobey authority.

X.   heating and hammering iron into different shapes.

Y.   the process of soaking animal hides in a solution to turn them into leather.

Z.   business that provides a certain product or service.

AA. a dangerous disease which causes fever and bumps all over the skin.

BB. took a person without permission.

CC. a disease the spreads quickly and affects many people at the same time.

DD. rich soil that produces a large number of crops.

EE. to change religions.

FF. established or set up.

GG. attacked suddenly.

Americans in California

You have already read about Spanish explorers in California and other areas in the West. Spain only controlled part of the land in America. France controlled the land along the western edge of the Mississippi River. Colonists from **Great Britain** controlled the land east of the Mississippi River.

In 1776, while the Spanish missionaries were busy building missions and rancherias in California, the colonists east of the Mississippi River were fighting for freedom from Great Britain. The colonists won the war and named themselves the United States of America. The United States was growing very quickly and needed more land. France and Spain controlled the land that the United States needed.

THE LOUISIANA PURCHASE

In 1803, France agreed to sell its land, known as the Louisiana Territory, to the United States. The sale of the Louisiana Territory became known as the Louisiana Purchase.

The Louisiana Purchase cost the United States 15 million dollars and added 800,000 square miles of land to the United States. This almost doubled the size of the United States and gave the United States complete control of the Mississippi River.

At only four cents per acre, the Louisiana Purchase was a good deal for the United States. The map on the left shows what the United States looked like back in the 1800s.

As you can see, Spain still controlled most of the land west of the Louisiana Purchase, including the land we now call California.

When we look at a map of the United States today, we see that it is divided into 50 sections, or states. If you have a map of the United States in your classroom, ask your teacher to pull it down for you so you can see that California is part of these 50 states. In the early 1800s, California was not even mentioned on the map. Have you ever wondered how California finally became part of the United States? To find the answer to this question, we need to travel back to the 1800s.

CONTROL OF CALIFORNIA

By the early 1800s, Spain had controlled California for almost 300 years. Spanish priests and soldiers built 21 missions along California's coast where Native Americans lived and worked. You have already read that Spain went to war with Mexico. Spain lost the war, and in 1821, the Mexican government took control of California.

In 1834, the missions were **disbanded.** A small part of the land was given back to the Native Americans. Many Mexican and a few American settlers entered California and purchased land from the Native Americans. The Mexican government took some of the mission land and gave it to Mexican ranchers. The land deals were not always fair and the Native Americans soon found themselves homeless. Many of them returned to work on the ranches for food and a place to sleep.

AMERICAN MOUNTAIN MEN

Beginning in 1825, settlers from the United States began traveling west into Mexican owned territory. American fur trappers and traders traveled from the town of Independence in Missouri, to the town of Santa Fe, New Mexico. They became known as mountain men. The mountain men searched for valuable beaver to trap and skin.

Beaver skins were very popular in the United States. The mountain men could earn a lot of money by hunting the beaver and taking the skins back to the United States. The beaver skins were used in the United States and **Europe** to make expensive beaver hats.

THE LIFE OF A MOUNTAIN MAN

The life of a mountain man was difficult. To survive in the wilderness, mountain men had to look like Native Americans. They dressed, walked, and even wore their hair like Native Americans. They traveled through all kinds of weather and fought off wild animals and attacks from unfriendly Native Americans.

Everything that a mountain man owned had to be carried with him. He traveled by horse and could only pack supplies that his horse could carry. One hand guided the horse while the other hand held a rifle. Gunpowder, a bullet pouch, an axe, a sharp knife, beaver traps, blankets, food, and cooking supplies were rolled up in a small bundle and strapped to the horse.

Most of the beaver furs were taken back to the United States where they were sold and made into hats. A few of the furs were sold at trading posts so the mountain men could buy flour, salt, coffee, tobacco, and more trapping supplies.

FAST FACTS

- James Ohio Pattie was a trapper who traveled to California. During his daring journeys he fought with Native Americans, was thrown in a Mexican jail, and even ate his dog to keep from starving.

The Santa Fe Trail

The route traveled by the mountain men became known as the Santa Fe Trail. The Santa Fe Trail was 800 miles long and started in Independence, Missouri. The trail snaked through Kansas, Colorado, and ended in Santa Fe, New Mexico. The mountain men knew there was more land to explore, so they began making the journey past the city of Santa Fe and into territories farther west. They were willing to brave harsh conditions and Native American attacks in order to explore, hunt, trap, and trade.

In 1826, mountain man Jedediah Smith became the first American to reach California by land. Other trappers and traders soon followed Smith across the dry Southwest deserts into California. They included Kit Carson, James Ohio Pattie, Joseph Reddeford Walker, and Ewing Young. Over the next few years, more mountain men and a few brave American settlers entered California. The Mexican government became fearful that the United States would try to take control of California and Mexico's other territory in the West.

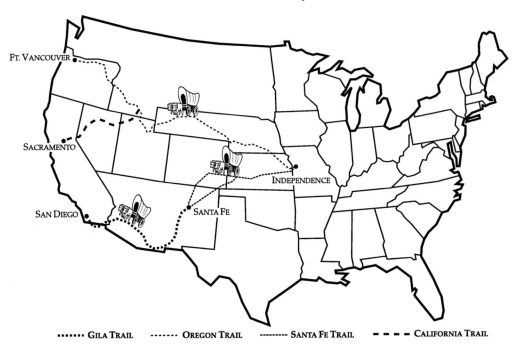

•••••• Gila Trail   ------- Oregon Trail   --------- Santa Fe Trail   – – – California Trail

Other Routes to California

Mexico had good reason to be worried. The United States government was interested in Mexico's land, especially the land in California. In 1841, John Bidwell led the first group of **pioneers** overland to California along what became known as the Oregon and California trails.

Thousands of pioneers followed Bidwell. Those who survived the 2000-mile long journey were rewarded with fertile farmland and wide open spaces. American settlers in California wanted the land to become part of the United States.

In 1846, the United States government sent Captain Philip Cooke to Santa Fe. Captain Cooke and his group of **Mormon** soldiers were instructed to find a route from Santa Fe to San Diego, California. The route, which was first traveled by Native Americans and Arizona missionary Father Kino, became known as the Gila Trail. It was 1,000 miles long and stretched through the Arizona desert, along the banks of the Colorado River, and into the steep mountains of California. The Gila Trail put the United States one step closer to its desire for control of California.

AMERICANS IN CALIFORNIA

Directions: Read each question carefully. Darken the circle for the correct answer.

1   The United States is divided into –

A   48 states

B   52 states

C   50 states

D   30 states

2   After studying the 1800s map, you can tell that –

F   the United States was located south of New Spain

G   California was part of the United States

H   the Louisiana Purchase included all of California

J   the United States was located east of the Louisiana Purchase

3   Which country took control of California in 1821?

A   The United States

B   Mexico

C   Spain

D   France

4   In 1834, the missions were disbanded and Native American families were given small pieces of land. Disbanded means –

F   broken up; separated

G   put back together

H   violent argument

J   on the outside

5   Mountain Men who traveled through Mexican owned territory on the Santa Fe Trail were searching for –

A   gold and silver

B   beaver furs

C   land to discover and control

D   water

6   Where did the Santa Fe Trail begin?

F   New York City

G   Los Angeles, California

H   Santa Fe, Canada

J   Independence, Missouri

7   To survive in the wilderness, Mountain Men –

A   had to look like Native Americans

B   ate bacon and eggs for breakfast

C   stopped every five miles to feed and water their horses

D   dressed like American soldiers

8   All of the following routes led to the West except –

F   the Santa Fe Trail

G   the Oregon Trail

H   the St. Louis Trail

J   the Gila Trail

READING

Answers

1 Ⓐ Ⓑ Ⓒ Ⓓ   5 Ⓐ Ⓑ Ⓒ Ⓓ

2 Ⓕ Ⓖ Ⓗ Ⓙ   6 Ⓕ Ⓖ Ⓗ Ⓙ

3 Ⓐ Ⓑ Ⓒ Ⓓ   7 Ⓐ Ⓑ Ⓒ Ⓓ

4 Ⓕ Ⓖ Ⓗ Ⓙ   8 Ⓕ Ⓖ Ⓗ Ⓙ

John Bidwell was born in New York on August 5, 1819. At the age of ten he moved with his parents to Erie, Pennsylvania. Two years later, the Bidwell family moved again, this time to Ashtabula, Ohio. John received a college education and became a teacher. He taught for a few years in Ohio before moving to Westport, Missouri. He bought a small farm in the area and continued teaching.

In 1840, John traveled to St. Louis, Missouri for a vacation. When he returned home, he found that a local **outlaw** had taken over his farm. John went straight to the sheriff, but the sheriff was too afraid of the outlaw to remove him from John's land. It was then that John made plans to leave Missouri.

John had read about a beautiful place known as California. He formed a club called the Western **Emigration** Society and advertised in the local newspaper that he was planning to take a large wagon train to California. He soon had the names of 500 people who were interested in taking this trip.

Bidwell knew that traveling to California was dangerous. He had heard the reports of brave mountain men who had made the difficult journey over the Rocky Mountains. Many had lost their lives. Still, John believed that finding a place with wide open spaces, beautiful weather, and good farm land was worth the risk.

THE JOURNEY TO CALIFORNIA

On May 9, 1841, the first wagon train to make the journey to California left Missouri. There were about 70 people in the party, but only five of them were women. The group was guided by Tom Fitzpatrick, an experienced mountain man who had successfully made the journey over the Rocky Mountains. Fitzpatrick agreed to take Bidwell's group as far as Oregon.

The six month journey taken by Bidwell's wagon train was a difficult one. The group ran out of food while crossing the Rocky Mountains. They had to leave their wagons and oxen and make part of the journey on foot. More than half of Bidwell's party died along the way. On November 4, 1841, a group of 32 became the first people to travel from Missouri to the Pacific Coast.

In California, John Bidwell went to work for John Sutter. In 1848, Bidwell discovered gold on the banks of the Feather River. His discovery made him a very wealthy man. The next year, at the age of 30, John Bidwell bought 22,000 acres of land near Sacramento.

In 1865, John began building a 26-room **mansion** that still stands today. He met and married Annie Ellicott Kennedy while the mansion was being built. Together they finished the $56,000 project that included gas lighting, indoor plumbing, marble furniture, and carpeting.

John Bidwell died on April 4, 1900, at the age of 81. He was a brave man who will always be remembered for leading the first wagon train from Missouri to California.

FAMOUS PEOPLE: JOHN BIDWELL

Directions: Use the selection about John Bidwell to answer these questions. Circle the answers to questions 1 and 2. Write your answers on the lines provided for questions 3-6.

---

1   According to the selection, John Bidwell made plans to move to California after –

   A he got married

   B he worked for John Sutter

   C his farm in Missouri was stolen

   D he turned 30 years old

2   After reading about John Bidwell, you get the idea that –

   A he was unable to find any gold in California

   B he was willing to risk his life for change

   C he was afraid to travel

   D he never got married

3   Why do you think so few women made the journey to California with Bidwell's group? If you had been a woman back then, would you have gone? Give reasons for your answer.

   _____

   _____

   _____

4   Are John Bidwell's accomplishments still important to us today? Explain your answer.

   _____

   _____

5   If you had survived the trip to California and then discovered gold, what would you have done with your money?

   _____

   _____

6   John Bidwell is remembered for being the first person to lead a group of pioneers from Missouri to California. What are you going to be remembered for?

   _____

   _____

MOUNTAIN MAN STORY

Have you ever wondered what it would have been like to live back in the 1800s, and explore the West like mountain men Jedediah Smith, James Ohio Pattie, and Ewing Young?

In this activity, you will travel back in time and write a story about when the West was an unsettled and dangerous place to explore.

DIRECTIONS:
- Before beginning your story, organize your thoughts by answering the five questions below.
- Write your rough draft on separate paper and have it edited. Make sure you include all of the details from the five questions you answered.
- Write your final draft on the special paper provided by your teacher. Attach extra paper if you need more space.
- Be prepared to read your story aloud to the rest of the class!

1. Describe who you were and what you looked like. _____

_____

_____

2. Explain your reason for traveling through the West. _____

_____

_____

3. Describe one dangerous or exciting event you faced along your journey. _____

_____

_____

_____

4. How did you survive in a place where Native American attacks were so common? ____

_____

_____

5. Will we read about you someday? If so, how did you become famous? _____

_____

_____

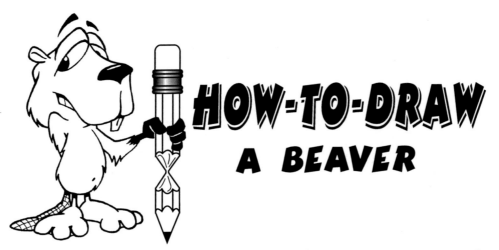

HOW-TO-DRAW
A BEAVER

During the late 1700s and 1800s, mountain men made the dangerous journey into the West in search of fur bearing animals like beaver. The skins were used in the United States and Europe to make expensive fur hats. By the late 1850s, the fur trade ended. Beaver hats were replaced with silk hats as the newest fashion in Europe. In this activity, you will follow written directions to draw a beaver.

DIRECTIONS: Very lightly sketch out the first step. Then, also very lightly add step 2. Continue in this way until all four steps are completed. In each drawing, the new step is shown darker than the step before it so that the lines can be clearly seen. You should keep your drawing very light.

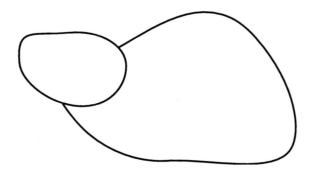

1. Draw these shapes to form the head and body.

2. Add lines to form the legs, the feet, and the tail.

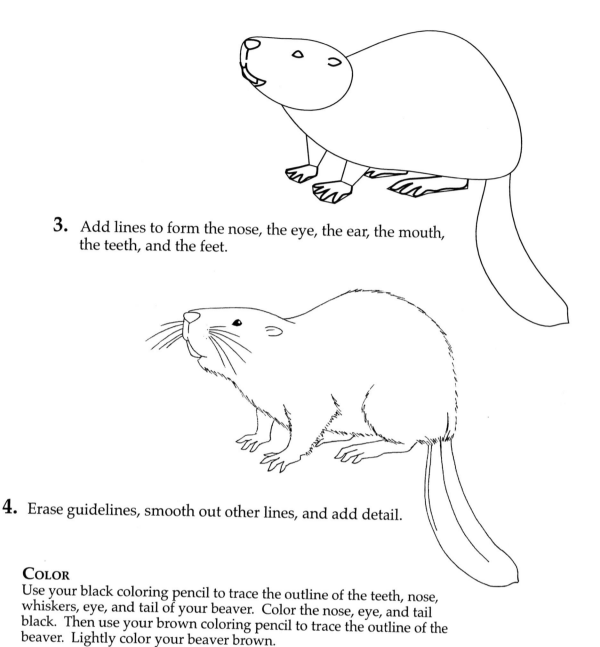

3. Add lines to form the nose, the eye, the ear, the mouth, the teeth, and the feet.

4. Erase guidelines, smooth out other lines, and add detail.

COLOR

Use your black coloring pencil to trace the outline of the teeth, nose, whiskers, eye, and tail of your beaver. Color the nose, eye, and tail black. Then use your brown coloring pencil to trace the outline of the beaver. Lightly color your beaver brown.

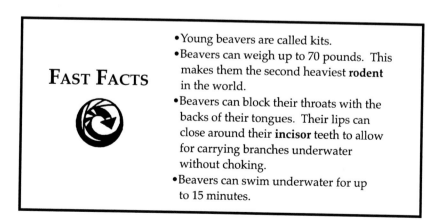

FAST FACTS

- Young beavers are called kits.
- Beavers can weigh up to 70 pounds. This makes them the second heaviest **rodent** in the world.
- Beavers can block their throats with the backs of their tongues. Their lips can close around their **incisor** teeth to allow for carrying branches underwater without choking.
- Beavers can swim underwater for up to 15 minutes.

THE MEXICAN WAR

There are only two ways to take over a territory: buy it like the United States did with the Louisiana Purchase, or win it in a war. In 1846, twenty five years after the creation of the Santa Fe Trail, the United States became interested in taking control of Mexico's land in the West. The United States was especially interested in California. The Mexican government refused to sell California to the United States.

Mexico and the United States also argued over **boundaries**. The two countries could not agree on the southern boundary of Texas. It seemed that the only way to gain more land and settle the boundary **dispute** was to go to war. On April 24, 1846, the United States declared war on Mexico.

THE BEAR FLAG REVOLT

Even before the first shots of the Mexican War were fired, the American settlers in California had dreams of claiming California for themselves. Two months after the beginning of the Mexican War, the American settlers took over the Mexican fort at Sonoma, north of San Francisco. They were led by former map maker and explorer John C. Frémont. The group quickly stitched together a flag with a grizzly bear and a star on it. They called themselves the California **Republic** and chose William B. Ide to be their president.

The California Republic lasted just one short month. In July, 1846, the United States Navy forced the settlers to raise the American flag over the area. Mexico fought back and regained control of California for a short time.

AMERICAN VICTORIES

Though Mexico was better prepared for war, the American troops had stronger leaders and **superior** equipment. From 1846 to 1847, the United States won almost every battle fought. American armies, led by famous men like Colonel Stephen Kearney, Kit Carson, John C. Frémont, Captain Philip Cooke, and Pauline Weaver marched in and easily took over Santa Fe, California, Tucson, and other Mexican territories.

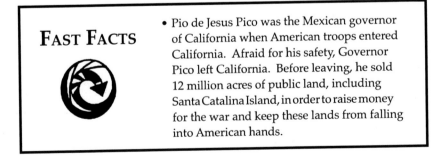

FAST FACTS

• Pio de Jesus Pico was the Mexican governor of California when American troops entered California. Afraid for his safety, Governor Pico left California. Before leaving, he sold 12 million acres of public land, including Santa Catalina Island, in order to raise money for the war and keep these lands from falling into American hands.

A Plan for Peace

Within a short time, Mexico had lost four times as many men in battle than the United States. In the spring of 1847, President James Polk sent Nicholas P. Trist to discuss a peace **treaty** with Mexico. President Polk hoped that this would end the war.

The president of Mexico refused to talk about peace with the United States. The Mexican War continued. In August, the United States Army marched into Mexico City and captured Mexico's capital. Mexico's president stepped down from power and a new government took control in Mexico. The new leaders feared that if they didn't sign the peace treaty with the United States, the war would continue and more Mexican land and lives would be lost.

The Treaty of Guadalupe-Hidalgo

On February 2, 1848, a peace treaty was signed between Mexico and the United States in the Mexican village of Guadalupe-Hidalgo. In this agreement, Mexico accepted the Rio Grande River as the southwestern boundary of Texas. Mexico also gave the United States its entire region of New Mexico. This included the western half of Colorado, northern half of Arizona, and the land the eventually became the states of California, Nevada, Utah, New Mexico, and Wyoming. In return, the United States paid Mexico 15 million dollars. Mexicans who already lived in the area were permitted to remain and become United States citizens.

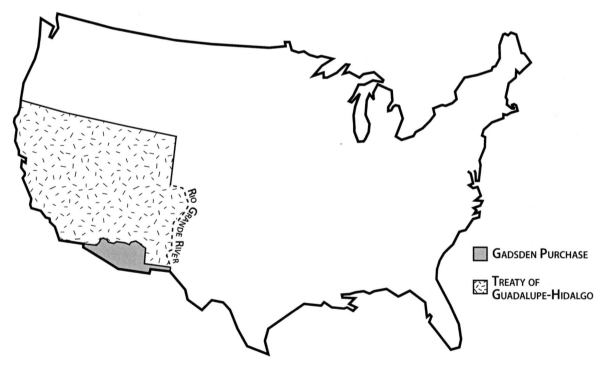

The Gadsden Purchase

In 1853, Mexico sold more land to the United States. This was known as the Gadsden Purchase. The United States paid 10 million dollars for 29,000 square miles of land. It included the southern half of Arizona and part of the present-day state of New Mexico. The boundaries of the United States were complete.

❧❧❧❧❧ THE MEXICAN WAR ❧❧❧❧❧

Directions: Read each question carefully. Darken the circle for the correct answer.

---

1 After reading the first paragraph of the Mexican War, you get the idea that –

   A the United States was not interested in taking control of Mexico's land

   B Mexico wanted to sell California

   C the United States planned to steal Mexico's land

   D Mexico wanted to keep California for itself

2 In the second paragraph, what does the word <u>dispute</u> mean?

   F peace

   G disagreement

   H friendliness

   J party

3 Why did Mexico's leaders finally decide to sign a peace treaty with the United States?

   A Mexico's leaders felt the United States deserved to win the war.

   B Mexico's leaders wanted to continue fighting the United States.

   C Mexico's leaders didn't want to lose any more land or lives.

   D Mexico's leaders planned to steal the land back from the United States.

4 Why was the peace treaty named the Treaty of Guadalupe-Hidalgo?

   F It was signed in the village of Guadalupe-Hidalgo.

   G It was named after Mexican soldiers Guadalupe and Hidalgo.

   H It was named after President Guadalupe-Hidalgo.

   J It was signed on the Mexican holiday Guadalupe-Hidalgo Day.

5 The Treaty of Guadalupe-Hidalgo included all of these future states <u>except</u> –

   A California

   B North Dakota

   C Utah

   D New Mexico

6 What can you learn from studying the map of the Guadalupe-Hidalgo Treaty and the Gadsden Purchase?

   F The Rio Grande River is south of the Gadsden Purchase.

   G The area of land bought in the Gadsden Purchase is larger than the land given in the Treaty of Guadalupe-Hidalgo.

   H The Gadsden Purchase is north of the Rio Grande River.

   J The Rio Grande River forms the eastern boundaries of the Treaty of Guadalupe-Hidalgo and the Gadsden Purchase.

7 Which of these statements about the Gadsden Purchase is <u>true</u>?

   A It added 29,000 square miles of land to the United States.

   B The Gadsden Purchase cost the United States 15 million dollars.

   C The Gadsden Purchase included the northern half of Arizona.

   D The land from the Gadsden Purchase became the California Territory.

READING

Answers

1 Ⓐ Ⓑ Ⓒ Ⓓ	5 Ⓐ Ⓑ Ⓒ Ⓓ
2 Ⓕ Ⓖ Ⓗ Ⓙ	6 Ⓕ Ⓖ Ⓗ Ⓙ
3 Ⓐ Ⓑ Ⓒ Ⓓ	7 Ⓐ Ⓑ Ⓒ Ⓓ
4 Ⓕ Ⓖ Ⓗ Ⓙ	

The Mexican War

Have you ever wondered what it would have been like to be alive during the Mexican War? What part do you think you would have played in the war? Maybe you would have been a soldier, fighting on the front line. Or maybe you would have been a commander like Colonel Stephen Kearney or Kit Carson. Perhaps you would have been a doctor or nurse caring for the wounded, or a Native American fighting for your land. Imagine the stories you would have to tell your friends and family when you returned from the war.

DIRECTIONS: Pretend you are part of the Mexican War. Decide what part you play in the war. Write a letter to someone back home. Tell them about your adventures. Make sure that your letter includes:

HEADING: Write your name on the first line, your address on the second line, and the date on the third line. (Remember, it's 1846.)

GREETING: This is where you write the name of the person to whom you are writing. The Greeting usually starts with Dear _____ and always ends with a comma.

BODY: This is where you write your letter. The first sentence of the Body is always indented a few spaces.

CLOSING: This is where you end your letter. The Closing should match the type of letter you are writing. If the letter is to someone you don't know very well, you might use Sincerely or Best Regards. If the letter is to a friend, you might use Your Friend or Love. The Closing always ends with a comma.

SIGNATURE: This is the official end to your letter when you sign your name. The Signature is always in cursive.

- Before beginning your letter, organize your thoughts by answering the four questions on the next page.
- Write your rough draft on separate paper and have it edited.
- Write your final draft on the special paper provided by your teacher.
- When you are finished with your final draft, place it in the envelope that your teacher will give you. Properly address the envelope.
- Be prepared to read your letter aloud to the rest of the class!

1. Describe who you were and what part you played in the Mexican War. _____

_____

_____

_____

2. List two historical facts about the Mexican War that you will include in your letter.

   a. _____

   _____

   _____

   Where did you find this fact? _____

   b. _____

   _____

   _____

   Where did you find this fact? _____

3. Describe an exciting or dangerous event that you will include in your letter. _____

_____

_____

_____

4. Who will you send your letter to? Explain why you have chosen this person.

_____

_____

_____

DIRECTIONS:

- Use your scissors to cut out the envelope along the **bold** black lines.
- Fold the envelope along the dotted black lines.
- Slip your letter inside the envelope, and seal the back of it with a single piece of tape or a sticker.

- Turn the envelope so the stamp is in the upper right-hand corner. Write the address of the person the letter is going to in the center of the envelope.
- Put your return address in the upper left-hand corner of the envelope.

TERRITORIAL DAYS

California did not automatically become a state after the Mexican War. The land that would one day become the state of California had been won in the war and granted to the United States in the Treaty of Guadalupe-Hidalgo. The Bear Flag Revolt had already proven that the settlers in California were ready to set up their own government. Still, the population of California was not large enough. The United States government required a territory to have 40,000 residents before applying for statehood. In 1848, the population of California was only 14,000. Most of these people were farmers and ranchers.

THE GOLD RUSH

In 1848, just a few months before the Treaty of Guadalupe-Hidalgo ended the Mexican War, something happened that would change the history of California forever. John Sutter, the man who purchased Fort Ross from the Russians, was having a sawmill built on his property. He hired a **carpenter** named James Marshall to be in charge of the construction. Mr. Marshall and his crew were building the sawmill on the American River, near present-day Sacramento. It was there, in the muddy waters of the American River, that James Marshall found gold nuggets.

John Sutter tried to keep James Marshall's discovery quiet. He did not want people entering his land to search for gold. Within a few months, the secret was out. Most of Sutter's workers left him in search of their own fortunes. Sutter was unable to keep hundreds of **prospectors** from trampling his land, destroying his crops, and killing his cattle. People all around him were "striking it rich," but John Sutter lost everything and died a poor man.

Within a year of James Marshall's gold discovery, thousands of people from the United States and other countries traveled to California to claim a piece of California's gold for themselves and hopefully become rich. Gold-seekers from Australia, New Zealand, Hawaii, and China traveled across the ocean by boat. Prospectors from the United States and Mexico arrived on horseback and in covered wagons. Nearly 100,000 people traveled to California during that first year. Because the year was 1849, they became known as the "Forty Niners."

FAST FACTS

- Overland travelers who made the journey from Missouri to California used oxen, horses, and mules to pull their wagons.
- The most popular animals for pulling the wagons were oxen. They were cheaper, stronger, and easier to work with than horses or mules. Mules cost $75.00 each, but an ox could be purchased for $25.00.
- Oxen were also less likely to be stolen by Native Americans on the journey and they made good farm animals once the wagons arrived in California.

MINING FOR GOLD

In the beginning of the Gold Rush, miners "panned" for gold by scooping pans with screen bottoms into the muddy waters of California's rivers and streams. The holes in the screens were big enough to let sand fall through, but small enough to stop any flakes of gold large enough to have value.

Later, the miners used a method known as cradle rocking to search for gold. They scooped up the mud, sand, and water from the bottom of the river and dumped it into a box with a screen bottom. They rocked the box back and forth to separate the gold from the mud and sand.

After the gold in and around the streams had been removed, miners turned their attention to the land around the river. Hard-rock miners used picks and axes to dig **shafts** and tunnels that were up to 40 feet deep to remove the gold. Ox-drawn wagons carried supplies into the mines and gold out of the mines.

GOLD PROSPECTOR

CALIFORNIA'S GOLD RUSH TOWNS

In 1848, before James Marshall's gold discovery, there were a few hundred people living in San Francisco. After gold was discovered, San Francisco became the starting place for most miners hoping to strike it rich during California's Gold Rush. Wagon trains and ships loaded with supplies and eager miners started their golden journeys in San Francisco. By 1850, San Francisco's population had grown to 25,000.

From San Francisco, miners traveled to the towns of Sacramento or Stockton. These towns became the center of activity for prospectors heading to the northern and southern mines. After a long week panning for gold, miners returned to one of these towns for a hot meal, a warm bed, entertainment, and new supplies for the next week. Everything could be purchased with gold nuggets or bags of gold dust.

LOUISE CLAPP

Most of the people in California's Gold Rush towns were men. On January 11, 1850, Louise Clapp arrived in San Francisco with her husband. While her husband traveled on to a digging site near the Feather River, Louise settled in Marysville. Marysville was a supply town for miners to go to at the end of the week. It was here that Louise wrote the first of 23 letters to her sister Molly, who lived in Massachusetts.

Louise's letters gave a woman's view of life during California's Gold Rush. She wrote about the beauty of the area and the noisy machines used to remove the nuggets of gold from the ground. She reported seeing miners of every color who spoke many different languages. Each of her letters was published in the local newspaper under the name Dame Shirley. She chose this name to keep her real name and identity a secret. In 1922, Louise Clapp's letters were published for the first time in a book.

Gold Rush Mining Camps

After the first discovery along the American River, gold was discovered in the **tributaries** (TRIB•yoo•tair•reez) of the Sacramento and San Joaquin (wah•KEEN) rivers. Other gold discoveries were made around the Trinity, Klamath, and Salmon rivers. Temporary towns, known as mining camps, were built near the mines. Gold miners lived in tents and wooden shacks where they survived on salt pork, biscuits, and molasses.

Hundreds of mining camps were created. In just a few short years, more than 465 million dollars worth of gold was mined in California. As these mining camps grew into towns, store owners with supplies were needed. Doctors, nurses, lawyers, ministers, and teachers soon arrived in California's new towns.

Unfortunately, not everyone found gold in California's mines. It was difficult work that required a lot of patience and money. When a miner thought he had discovered gold, he filed a claim giving him the right to mine and take all of the gold he found. It was impossible to do all of the work by himself, so the claim holder hired miners to dig holes, lift large stones, and remove the gold. Sometimes it took months and even years to actually find and remove the gold. During this time, the claim holder was responsible for paying his workers and supplying them with food, picks, shovels, pans, and mules. Most of the time the claim holder went broke before any gold was actually found and removed.

Territorial Sheriff

California's Outlaws

Many people who failed to find gold stayed in California and became wheat farmers, cattle and sheep ranchers, or opened businesses in California's territorial towns. As the population of California grew, the need for law **enforcement** became important.

Not everyone who settled in California was interested in making it a safe place to live. Robberies, fights, and other acts of violence were frequent. Each mining town had to have its own sheriff to protect the town's people and punish the criminals. This wasn't always enough, and by the beginning of 1850, Californians hoped that statehood and an organized government would come soon.

Fast Facts

- Dr. Jerry Crane and Mickey Free were the first two criminals hanged in California.
- Both men were found guilty of murder and hanged on the same day in the middle of the town square. A huge crowd watched the double hanging. The sheriff even hired a band to entertain those watching the event.

❧❧❧❧❧ TERRITORIAL DAYS ❧❧❧❧❧

Directions: Read each question carefully. Darken the circle for the correct answer.

---

1 After the Mexican War, California became –

   A a state

   B a city

   C a country

   D a territory

2 Why were California's gold prospectors known as "Forty Niners?"

   F They came to California in 1849.

   G Every prospector was 49 years old.

   H It took 49 days for prospectors to remove gold from the mines.

   J There were only 49 people in California at the beginning of the Gold Rush.

3 James Marshall found nuggets of gold near –

   A San Francisco

   B Sacramento

   C Lake Tahoe

   D San Diego

4 After reading about how prospectors mined for gold, you get the idea that –

   F large trucks were used to remove the gold from the mines

   G miners always used the cradle rocking method to search for gold

   H Panning for gold was the only method used to search for gold

   J gold could be found in and around many of California's streams and rivers

5 Which of the following statements about California's first territorial towns is **false**?

   A Gold nuggets were accepted as a form of payment for gold mining supplies in the territorial towns.

   B The population of San Francisco did not change during the Gold Rush.

   C San Francisco was the starting place for most miners hoping to strike it rich during the Gold Rush.

   D Before the discovery of gold, there were only a few hundred people living in San Francisco.

6 Which of these phrases best describes why gold miners did not always strike it rich?

   F ...more than 465 million dollars worth of gold...

   G ...claim holders went broke before any gold was actually found...

   H ...hundreds of mining camps were created...

   J ...hired miners to dig holes, lift large stones, and remove the gold...

7 Why did California's early towns need law enforcement?

   A Everyone who settled in California wanted to make it a safe place to live.

   B Stores opened that sold supplies to miners.

   C Robberies, fights, and other acts of violence were frequent.

   D Everyone always followed the rules.

READING

Answers

1 Ⓐ Ⓑ Ⓒ Ⓓ   5 Ⓐ Ⓑ Ⓒ Ⓓ

2 Ⓕ Ⓖ Ⓗ Ⓙ   6 Ⓕ Ⓖ Ⓗ Ⓙ

3 Ⓐ Ⓑ Ⓒ Ⓓ   7 Ⓐ Ⓑ Ⓒ Ⓓ

4 Ⓕ Ⓖ Ⓗ Ⓙ

The Santa Fe Trail

During the 1870s, thousands of pioneer families followed the Santa Fe Trail from Independence, Missouri into Santa Fe, New Mexico, and then into California. These families helped build California's first territorial towns. The journey along the Santa Fe Trail was a dangerous adventure that took four to six months. Pioneers faced many challenges along the Santa Fe Trail. Sickness, lack of food, Native American attacks, and bad weather were some of the things that kept many pioneers from reaching California.

This activity will give you a chance to experience life on the Santa Fe Trail. As you make the journey with your family, you will keep a record of your adventures in a **journal**. A **journal** is a written record of events. Fortunately, many pioneers kept journals while traveling the Santa Fe Trail. Without these **primary sources** from people who were actually there, we would have a difficult time learning about the past.

DIRECTIONS:

1. Cut out the sample page and six blank journal pages. (Cut on the dotted lines so that each full page makes two half pages. This will actually give you 14 pages.)

2. Cut out and neatly color the front and back covers for your journal. (Cut on the dotted lines so that you have two half pieces.)

3. Put your journal together. Put the front cover on top, the back cover on the bottom, and your 14 journal pages in between. (The first page of your journal should be the sample page with the picture. The second page should be the sample page with just the writing. Place your other blank pages in the journal the same way.)

4. Staple your journal together along the left side of the cover.

5. Choose six of the eight events pictured to write about. (You can choose to draw some or even all of your own pictures.)

6. Cut out and neatly color each event that you have chosen.

7. Paste each event on the journal pages that have the blank square. (If you're drawing your own pictures, draw them in the square.)

8. Write a journal entry for each event. As you write, keep in mind that each journal entry must be dated. The sample page starts your journal on April 1, 1870. The rest of your journal entries should be dated after April 1. Your journal should end the day you arrive in California.

April 1, 1870

Today is the first day of our journey West. My pa says it is the first day of the rest of our lives. I'm not exactly sure what that means, but I'm pretty excited anyway. We stopped in a town called Independence to pick up all of our supplies for the trip. We loaded up on everything!

Pa bought bullets for his gun, coffee, tobacco for his pipe, and two extra strings for his fiddle. Ma brought fruits and vegetables from our garden, four slabs of bacon from the hog we slaughtered, and plenty of corn flour for homemade biscuits. I don't think we will ever run out of food. Me? I'm just happy to have a seat in the wagon. I spent my money on a rattle for the new baby that Ma is going to have on the trip. I also bought four black licorice whips and two jaw breakers. To share, of course. I'm a little worried about making it safely to where we are going. I've heard stories of hostile Indians and snow covered mountains that are taller than any I've ever seen. My pa tells me that I worry too much about things that I can't change. I just hope that everyone in my family stays healthy and the oxen remain strong.

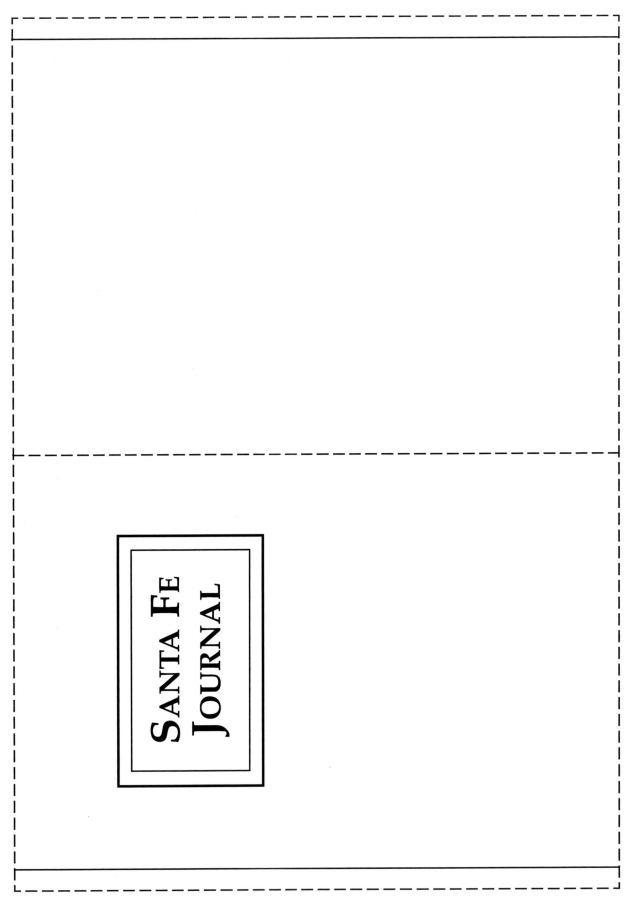

SANTA FE
JOURNAL

STATEHOOD

By the beginning of 1850, California had been a United States territory for two years. During that time, the population of California had grown from 14,000 to well over 100,000 people. Californians were becoming impatient. They wanted to join the United States so they could be involved in national decisions like making laws and deciding who would govern them and enforce those laws.

SLAVERY

While gold was being discovered in California, a battle was brewing in the United States over the issue of slavery. Since the early 1500s, slavery had been a part of America. Huge ships traveled to Africa where black men, women, and children were captured and taken to America. Once in America, they were sold as slaves to white farmers who forced them to work on their tobacco and cotton **plantations**.

The black slaves were the property of their owners, or masters. They worked in the fields from morning until night. Slaves were paid no money, often fed little food, and given poor clothing. They were not allowed to go to school or even learn to read and write. Their white masters could beat them at any time for any reason. If slaves had any children, they too belonged to their white masters.

A DIVIDED NATION

Many people in the United States disagreed with slavery. They felt it was wrong to own other human beings and force them to work without pay. The settlers who lived in the southern part of the United States argued that they needed slaves to work on their plantations. The settlers who lived in the northern part of the United States wanted slavery to end.

The leaders in Washington who made decisions for the United States knew it was important to keep the slave states and the free states balanced. There were already 30 states in the Union, equally divided between free and slave states. Adding California as a free state or a slave owning state would upset this balance.

THE COMPROMISE OF 1850

In 1850, **Congress** reached a **compromise** that it hoped would keep peace between the North and the South. The Compromise of 1850 permitted the new territories of New Mexico, Nevada, Arizona, and Utah to choose for themselves whether or not to allow slavery. It also permitted California to enter the Union as a free state. To keep slave owners happy, the Compromise of 1850 also included the Fugitive Slave Act. The Fugitive Slave Act required runaway slaves to be captured and returned to their plantations.

STATEHOOD

In September of 1849, one year before the Compromise of 1850, forty eight **delegates** met in Monterey to **draft** a state **constitution**. It outlined the laws of California and **prohibited** slavery. One year later, on September 9, 1850, California became the 31st state to join the Union. Just as the delegates had hoped, California was admitted as a free state. Peter H. Burnett was **elected** as California's first **governor**.

CALIFORNIA'S SYMBOLS

A new state is responsible for designing a flag and choosing symbols to represent

itself. Since the discovery of gold had played a major part in California's rush to statehood, it was nicknamed the Golden State. A state seal was designed and approved as the symbol of California. The state seal is stamped on all government papers to make them **official**.

In addition to a seal and a nickname, Californians chose the California quail as the state bird, the California poppy as the state flower, and the Giant redwood as the state tree. California's **motto** is "Eureka!" which means "I Found It!" This motto was chosen to represent the importance of California's gold discoveries.

In 1911, California's state flag was **adopted**. The flag is known as the Bear Flag. It is red and white with a red star in the left-hand corner and a grizzly bear in the center. The grizzly bear is California's state **mammal**. The red star and the words "California Republic" written at the bottom represent the flag used during the Bear Flag Revolt when the settlers of California declared themselves an independent nation.

FAST FACTS

- The California poppy is a flowering plant native to California and many regions of central Europe and southern France.
- It was once a valuable source of food for California's Native Americans. They also used the juices in the root of the California poppy to relieve toothaches and boiled the seeds to treat headaches.

THE CIVIL WAR

In 1860, ten years after California was admitted as a free state, Abraham Lincoln was elected president of the United States. President Lincoln promised to **abolish** slavery.

The Southern states refused to be told what to do by President Lincoln. They separated from the United States and formed a new nation. They called themselves the Confederate States of America. The Confederacy chose Jefferson Davis from Mississippi to be its president.

President Lincoln was **outraged** that the Southern states had split from the United States. He was willing to fight to put the United States back together and outlaw slavery. In 1861, the first shots of the Civil War were fired in South Carolina.

CALIFORNIA'S HELPS WIN THE WAR

As a free state, California stayed **loyal** to President Lincoln and the Union. Fortunately, no Civil War battles were actually fought in California, but California played an important role in the war.

Money from California's gold mines helped pay for the Civil War. Wheat from California's farms helped feed the soldiers. Wool from the state's sheep ranches kept the soldiers warm.

In addition, more than 15,000 volunteers from California fought in the Union Army. California's soldiers helped keep the land between California and the rest of the Union safe from **invasion** by the Confederate Army. Soldiers in California also guarded the Pacific Coast and kept the Confederacy from entering California.

In 1865, the Civil War ended. Slavery was abolished and the United States was made whole again. The Southern states were required to free their slaves and change the way they treated their black citizens. The Civil War only lasted four years, but it took much longer for these other changes to be made.

ABRAHAM LINCOLN

JEFFERSON DAVIS

FAST FACTS

• The United States Constitution guarantees that anyone **accused** of a crime receive fair treatment and a trial by a **jury**. The Fugitive Slave Act took this away from blacks all over the United States. Blacks who were captured were **denied** a trial. With no legal rights in the United States, more than 20,000 blacks ran away to live in Canada.

CALIFORNIA: THE 31ST STATE

Directions: Read each question carefully. Darken the circle for the correct answer.

---

1 While gold was being discovered in California, what issue was being discussed in the rest of the United States?

    A Cruelty to animals

    B Slavery

    C Transportation

    D Lack of water

2 What did California's state constitution say about slavery?

    F Slavery was not allowed in California.

    G Californians could choose for themselves about slavery.

    H Only Californians who lived in the southern part of the state could own slaves.

    J Slavery was permitted in California.

3 On what date did California become a state?

    A October 7, 1849

    B January 6, 1851

    C February 14, 1912

    D September 9, 1850

4 California's motto is "Eureka!" which means –

    F Good Luck!

    G Hello U.S.A.!

    H I Found It!

    J Gold!

5 What happened to the United States when Abraham Lincoln was elected president?

    A The Northern states separated from the United States.

    B Slavery became legal.

    C The United States went to war with Mexico.

    D The Southern state separated from the United States.

6 After reading about the Civil War, you get the idea that –

    F it lasted for nine years

    G the Civil War ended slavery in the United States

    H all of the Civil War battles were fought in California

    J the Southern states were permitted to keep their slaves after the Civil War ended

7 How many Civil War battles were fought in California?

    A 6

    B 15

    C 10

    D 0

READING

Answers

1 Ⓐ Ⓑ Ⓒ Ⓓ   5 Ⓐ Ⓑ Ⓒ Ⓓ

2 Ⓕ Ⓖ Ⓗ Ⓙ   6 Ⓕ Ⓖ Ⓗ Ⓙ

3 Ⓐ Ⓑ Ⓒ Ⓓ   7 Ⓐ Ⓑ Ⓒ Ⓓ

4 Ⓕ Ⓖ Ⓗ Ⓙ

On August 15, 1818, a baby girl was born to slave parents in Mississippi. Her name was Bridget Mason, but they called her "Biddy" for short. Because Biddy's parents were slaves, she was also a slave.

Traveling West

In 1847, Biddy's owner, Robert Smith, became a Mormon. He moved his family to the Utah Territory where Mormon pioneers were building a new community. Although Biddy was 29 years old with three children of her own, she and her children were still the property of Robert Smith. Biddy and her daughters, Ellen, Ann, and Harriet, made the 2,000 mile journey with the Smith family.

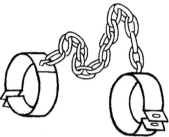

While the Smiths and their white children traveled by covered wagon, Biddy and her black children completed most of the trip on foot. During the six month journey, Biddy was responsible for herding the cattle, preparing the meals, delivering babies, and taking care of the children.

In 1851, Robert Smith decided once again to move his family and slaves. This time, he chose California where a new Mormon community was being settled. Biddy and her daughters, still the property of Mr. Smith, traveled to California.

Freedom From Slavery

Robert Smith probably didn't know that California had recently joined the Union as a free state. Slavery was **illegal** in California. In 1856, the state of California granted Biddy and her daughters freedom. They moved to Los Angeles, where Biddy worked as a nurse. Within ten years, Biddy had saved enough money to buy a piece of property and build a house. The purchase cost her $250.00 and made Biddy Mason one of the first black women to own property in Los Angeles. By selling some of her land and making wise business choices, Biddy was able to save more than $300,000 during her lifetime.

Biddy Mason was generous with her money and her time. She gave money to **charities**, visited people in jail, and provided food and shelter to many poor families in Los Angeles. When a flood struck Los Angeles, Biddy had food prepared for the flood victims and paid the bills herself. In 1872, Biddy and her son-in-law founded and paid for the First African Methodist Episcopal Church of Los Angeles. This was the city's first black church.

On January 15, 1891, Biddy Mason died at the age of 73. Like most black people who died during the 1800s, she was buried in an unmarked grave. Almost 100 years later, a tombstone was finally placed on her grave and a ceremony honoring her life was attended by the mayor of Los Angeles and 3,000 members of the First African Methodist Episcopal Church.

FAMOUS PEOPLE: BIDDY MASON

Directions: Use the selection about Biddy Mason to answer these questions. Circle the answers to questions 1 and 2. Write your answers on the lines provided for questions 3-6.

1   After reading about the Smith family in this selection, you get the idea that –

    A they were against slavery

    B they gave Biddy her freedom after she had children of her own

    C they were a religious family

    D they moved to California so Biddy and her children could be free from slavery

2   Biddy Mason was born in 1818 and she was granted freedom from slavery in 1856. How old was Biddy when she was granted her freedom?

    A 45

    B 32

    C 73

    D 38

3   Describe how Biddy's life as a slave makes you feel.

_____

_____

_____

4   Give three examples of positive things that Biddy Mason did in her life.

    a._____

    b. _____

    c._____

5   Why do you think Biddy Mason spent all of that time and energy helping other people?

_____

_____

6   If Biddy Mason was alive today, do you think she would be proud of the way black and white Americans treat each other? Give reasons for your answer.

_____

_____

_____

CALIFORNIA'S STATE FLAG

The Bear Flag was first raised on June 14, 1846, by a group of American settlers who revolted against Mexico and declared California as an independent nation. They called themselves the California Republic. Although it lasted only one month, the California Republic and the Bear Flag were not forgotten.

In 1911, California's state flag was adopted. Just like the Bear Flag, the state flag is red and white with a red star in the left-hand corner and a grizzly bear in the center. The grizzly bear is California's state mammal. Now **extinct**, the California grizzly bear was drawn on the flag to represent the large number of bears found in California. The red star and the words "California Republic" written at the bottom represent the flag used during the Bear Flag Revolt.

In this activity, you will follow directions to correctly color the California state flag on the next page.

DIRECTIONS:

1. Using your red coloring pencil, color the star and the wide strip along the bottom of the flag. The background of the flag should remain white.

2. Outline the grizzly bear using your dark brown coloring pencil. Use a lighter brown to color in the grizzly bear.

3. Color the patch of grass below the grizzly bear green.

CALIFORNIA'S STATE FLAG

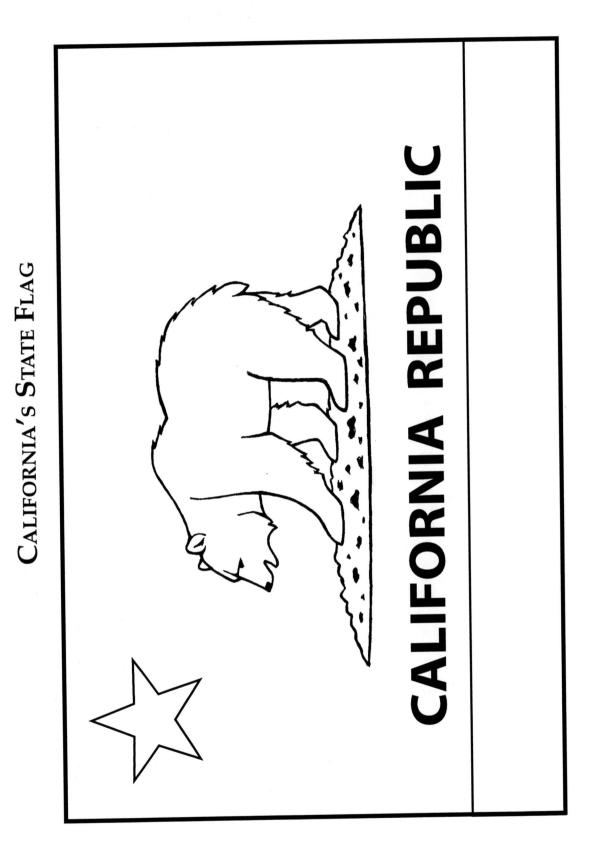

CALIFORNIA REPUBLIC

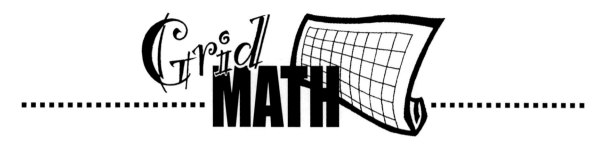

Grid MATH

Grid Math is a fun way to learn an important skill. Grids are used to find places on maps, to track weather patterns, and in space exploration.

FOR EXAMPLE: If you want to draw a box where C meets 3 (C,3), you would go <u>over</u> to C and <u>up</u> to 3, and draw the box in that space. On a map or an atlas, (C,3) may be the place where you would find the name of a city.

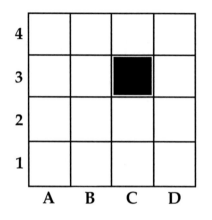

DIRECTIONS: In this activity you will use a grid system to put together a puzzle that should remind you of a California state symbol. You will need the 48 puzzle pieces (some of the puzzle pieces are below and the rest of them are on the next page), and the blank grid.

1. Cut out the puzzle pieces **one at a time** (cut around the thick black line of the square). Glue **that** piece in its proper place on the empty grid before cutting out the next piece. Make sure that you do not turn the puzzle piece upside down or turn it on its side before gluing it; the way it looks before you cut it out is the way it should be glued onto the grid.

2. Follow the example above: If the puzzle piece is labeled **(D,1)**, glue that piece in the space where D meets 1 on the grid by going <u>over</u> to D and <u>up</u> to 1.

3. When you are finished, color in your picture with your coloring pencils.

4. The first one has been done for you as an example.

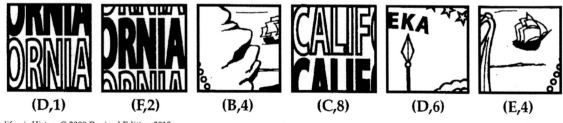

(D,1)   (F,2)   (B,4)   (C,8)   (D,6)   (E,4)

(E,7)   (B,8)   (C,2)   (D,5)   (C,6)   (A,6)

(C,5)   (D,2)   (E,8)   (A,4)   (C,7)   (E,3)

(F,7)   (B,5)   (F,5)   (A,2)   (C,4)   (B,7)

(E,6)   (A,8)   (F,6)   (B,3)   (C,1)   (E,2)

(F,8)   (D,4)   (F,1)   (A,7)   (B,2)   (D,3)

(E,5)   (F,3)   (A,1)   (B,6)   (E,1)   (D,7)

(C,3)   (A,5)   (F,4)   (B,1)   (A,3)   (D,8)

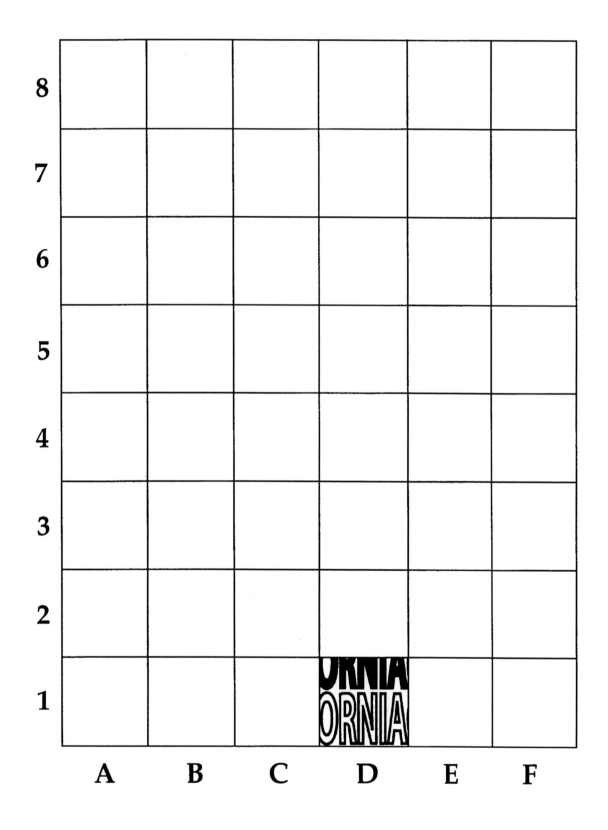

✦✦✦✦✦✦ VOCABULARY QUIZ ✦✦✦✦✦✦

CALIFORNIA HISTORY
PART IV

Directions: Match the vocabulary word on the left with its definition on the right. Put the letter for the definition on the blank next to the vocabulary word it matches. Use each word and definition only once.

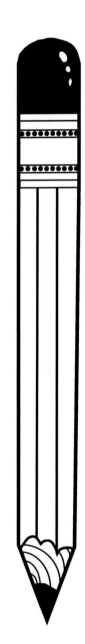

1. _____ disbanded

2. _____ boundaries

3. _____ carpenter

4. _____ abolish

5. _____ emigration

6. _____ mammal

7. _____ enforcement

8. _____ adopted

9. _____ Europe

10. _____ republic

11. _____ prospectors

12. _____ charities

13. _____ Great Britain

14. _____ superior

15. _____ shafts

16. _____ delegates

17. _____ incisor

18. _____ treaty

19. _____ tributaries

A. a skilled worker who makes and repairs objects made of wood.

B. refused to approve something.

C. long, narrow openings dug into the earth.

D. very large farms in the South where crops of cotton and tobacco were grown and slave labor was generally used.

E. early settlers who prepared the way for others to follow.

F. a short phrase describing conduct or principles.

G. a requirement of someone to obey the rules.

H. a surprise attack where force is used to enter and take control.

I. people who explore areas for gold or other minerals.

J. streams that flow into a larger body of water.

K. broken up; separated.

L. a group of people who are chosen to listen to all of the facts during a court case before making a judgment for guilt or innocence.

M. a person who belongs to a religious group that was founded in 1830, and traces its beginnings to Joseph Smith.

N. small mammal with large front teeth used for gnawing or nibbling.

O. an independent nation with its own form of government, usually a president.

P. accepted and put into action.

Q. the sixth smallest of Earth's seven continents.

R. proper or correct.

20. _____ extinct

21. _____ mansion

22. _____ elected

23. _____ Mormon

24. _____ governor

25. _____ outlaw

26. _____ illegal

27. _____ pioneers

28. _____ invasion

29. _____ rodent

30. _____ loyal

31. _____ prohibited

32. _____ motto

33. _____ official

34. _____ outraged

35. _____ plantations

36. _____ dispute

37. _____ draft

38. _____ compromise

39. _____ Congress

40. _____ jury

41. _____ denied

42. _____ constitution

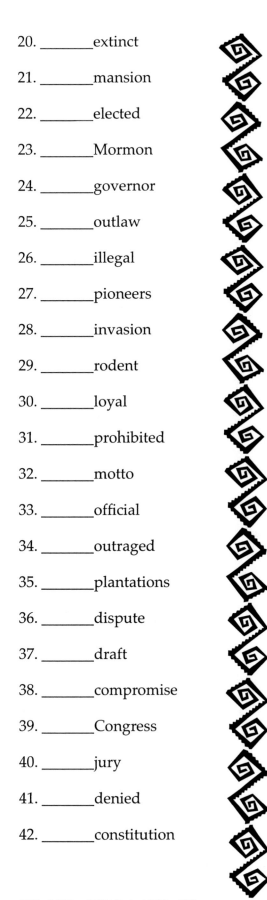

S.   men and women in the Senate and House of Representatives who are elected to make laws for the United States.

T.   dividing lines.

U.   stay committed to a person or a cause.

V.   people sent with power to represent others.

W.   a decision reached when each side gives up something in order to make the other side happy.

X.   one of four sharp-edged teeth in the front of the mouth used by mammals for cutting and gnawing.

Y.   a person who is in charge of an area or a group of people.

Z.   an action or behavior that is not permitted.

AA. better than the rest.

BB. argument or disagreement.

CC. to move away from one place and settle in another.

DD. the largest island in Europe. It includes England, Scotland, and Wales.

EE. a formal agreement.

FF. selected by voting.

GG. the plan for the state or nation that outlines the duties of government and guarantees the rights of the people.

HH. angered beyond belief.

II. types of groups that receive donations of money or gifts and give them to people in need.

JJ. warm-blooded animal that feeds its young with milk, has a backbone, and is covered with hair.

KK. no longer living.

LL. against the law.

MM. write.

NN. stop or put an end to.

OO. a person who breaks the law.

PP. huge home.

Glossary

ab•a•lo•ne a large sea creature that lives in an ear-shaped shell and clings closely to rocks.

a•ban•doned gave up completely.

a•bol•ish stop or put an end to.

a•dop•ted accepted and put into action.

ag•ri•cul•ture planting crops and raising farm animals.

al•lies groups of people who come together to help one another in times of trouble.

an•chored held a ship in place with a heavy metal object attached to a strong rope or cable.

aq•ue•ducts pipes that take water from one place to another.

ar•chae•ol•o•gists scientists who study past human life by looking at prehistoric fossils and tools.

A•sia the world's largest continent with more than half of the Earth's population.

at•tain•ing getting for oneself.

au•to•bi•og•ra•phy the story of your life written by you.

bi•og•ra•phies stories of a person's life written by someone else.

black•smith•ing heating and hammering iron into different shapes.

block•ade shutting off a place to keep people and supplies from coming in or going out.

bound•a•ries dividing lines.

bur•rows holes that are dug by small animals.

ca•nals man-made waterways for boats or for watering crops.

cap•i•tal the city that serves as the center of government for the state or nation.

cap•tive someone who is held without permission.

car•go freight carried by a ship.

car•pen•ter a skilled worker who makes and repairs objects made of wood.

cen•tu•ries periods of 100 years.

cer•e•mo•nies religious or spiritual gatherings.

chan•nel the deeper part of a waterway.

char•i•ties types of groups that receive donations of money or gifts and give them to people in need.

Chris•ti•an•i•ty a religion based on the life and teachings of Jesus Christ.

cit•i•zens people in a city, town, state, or country who enjoy the freedom to vote and participate in government decisions.

cli•mate the average condition of weather over a period of years.

coast an area of land that borders water.

col•o•nies groups of people who are ruled by another country.

com•pro•mise a decision reached when each side gives up something in order to make the other side happy.

Con•gress men and women in the Senate and House of Representatives who are elected to make laws for the United States.

con•quered took over by force.

con•sti•tu•tion the plan for the state or nation that outlines the duties of government and guarantees the rights of the people.

con•struc•tion work that involves putting something together.

con•ti•nent one of seven large areas of land on the globe.

con•vert to change religions.

con•vinced talked someone into doing something your way.

cul•ture a group of people who share a set of beliefs, goals, religious customs, attitudes, and social practices.

cur•rents quickly moving bodies of water.

customs usual ways of doing things.

de•feat•ing winning victory over.

del•e•gates people sent with power to represent others.

de•nied refused to approve something.

de•scen•dants family members who come after one has died.

dis•band•ed broken up; separated.

dis•pute argument or disagreement.

draft write.

dwel•lings houses.

e•lect•ed selected by voting.

em•i•gra•tion to move away from one place and settle in another.

em•per•or the male ruler of an empire.

em•pire a group of territories or peoples under one ruler.

en•force•ment a requirement of someone to obey the rules.

ep•i•dem•ic a disease the spreads quickly and affects many people at the same time.

Eu•rope the sixth smallest of Earth's seven continents.

ex•pand grow larger.

ex•tinct no longer living.

fer•tile rich soil that produces a large number of crops.

fer•til•ized added a material to the soil to make crops grow better.

for•eign from another country.

for•mer coming from the past.

found•ed established or set up.

gov•er•nor a person who is in charge of an area or a group of people.

grants gifts of land.

Great Bri•tain the largest island in Europe. It includes England, Scotland, and Wales.

har•bors sheltered parts of water deep enough to provide ships a place to anchor.

harsh strict and sometimes unfair treatment.

hearth the floor of a fireplace that is covered with brick or cement and usually stretches into a room.

his•to•ri•ans people who study history.

hoax a trick.

il•le•gal against the law.

in•ci•sor one of four sharp-edged teeth in the front of the mouth used by mammals for cutting and gnawing.

in•de•pen•dence not under the control or rule of another.

in•dus•try business that provides a certain product or service.

in•hab•it•ed lived or settled in a place.

in•trud•ers people who enter without permission.

in•va•sion a surprise attack where force is used to enter and take control.

ir•ri•gate water crops by digging a ditch that leads from a body of water to a farm.

ju•ry a group of people who are chosen to listen to all of the facts during a court case before making a judgment for guilt or innocence.

kid•napped took a person without permission.

knight a title given to a man who has done something very special for England.

live•stock animals raised on a farm to eat or sell for profit.

loy•al stay committed to a person or a cause.

mam•mal warm-blooded animal that feeds its young with milk, has a backbone, and is covered with hair.

man•sion huge home.

mis•sions types of churches.

Mor•mon a person who belongs to a religious group that was founded in 1830, and traces its beginnings to Joseph Smith.

mot•to a short phrase describing conduct or principles.

North A•mer•i•ca one of seven continents in the world. Bounded by Alaska on the northwest, Greenland on the northeast, Florida on the southeast, and Mexico on the southwest.

of•fi•cial proper or correct.

or•chards groups of fruit trees.

out•law a person who breaks the law.

out•raged angered beyond belief.

pi•o•neers early settlers who prepared the way for others to follow.

plan•ta•tions very large farms in the South where crops of cotton and tobacco were grown and slave labor was generally used.

priest person with the authority to perform religious ceremonies.

prof•it•a•ble a type of business that makes more money than it spends.

pro•hib•it•ed an action or behavior that is not permitted.

pros•pec•tors people who explore areas for gold or other minerals.

pros•per•ous having success or wealth.

quad•ran•gle a rectangular area surrounded on all sides by buildings.

raid•ed attacked suddenly.

ran•che•ri•as small villages of Native American settlements.

ran•som money paid for the safe return of a person who has been taken without permission.

re•bel disobey authority.

rec•re•a•tion•al a type of activity designed for rest and relaxation.

re•cruit to find people who are willing to join a military force.

re•pub•lic an independent nation with its own form of government, usually a president.

re•sourc•es things found in nature that are valuable to humans.

ro•dent small mammal with large front teeth used for gnawing or nibbling.

sac•ri•ficed killed an animal or human being as a spiritual offering.

sculp•tures figures or designs shaped out of clay, marble, or metal.

shafts long, narrow openings dug into the earth.

shal•low a hole that is not very deep.

small•pox a dangerous disease which causes fever and bumps all over the skin.

sub•merged partly below ground or underwater.

su•pe•ri•or better than the rest.

tal•low a white solid fat produced by heating the fatty tissues of cattle and sheep and used for making candles and soap.

tan•ning the process of soaking animal hides in a solution to turn them into leather.

tem•po•rar•y lasting for a short period of time.

trea•ty a formal agreement.

trib•u•tar•ies streams that flow into a larger body of water.

tule a large plant that grows in the swampy areas of California with long flat leaves that are used for making mats and chair seats.

voy•age journey usually made by water.

ANSWERS TO COMPREHENSION QUESTIONS

CALIFORNIA'S FIRST PEOPLE

1. C
2. G
3. A
4. J
5. B
6. H
7. D

CALIFORNIA'S EXPLORERS

1. C
2. J
3. C
4. G
5. A
6. J
7. C

SPANISH MISSIONS

1. B
2. J
3. C
4. J
5. A
6. H
7. D

AMERICANS IN CALIFORNIA

1. C
2. J
3. B
4. F
5. B
6. J
7. A
8. H

FAMOUS PEOPLE: JOHN BIDWELL

1. C
2. B
3. Answers will vary
4. Answers will vary
5. Answers will vary
6. Answers will vary

THE MEXICAN WAR

1. D
2. G
3. C
4. F
5. B
6. J
7. A

TERRITORIAL DAYS

1. D
2. F
3. B
4. J
5. B
6. G
7. C

CALIFORNIA: THE 31ST STATE

1. B
2. F
3. D
4. H
5. D
6. G
7. D

FAMOUS PEOPLE: BIDDY MASON

1. C
2. D
3. Answers will vary
4. Proved that a woman could do well in business; gave money to charities; visited people in jail; fed and sheltered poor people; used her own money to help flood victims; founded and paid for Los Angeles's first black church.
5. Answers will vary
6. Answers will vary

ANSWERS TO VOCABULARY QUIZZES

PART I	PART II	PART III	PART IV
1. H	1. I	1. Y	1. K
2. A	2. Z	2. K	2. T
3. R	3. V	3. U	3. A
4. M	4. P	4. N	4. NN
5. V	5. X	5. AA	5. CC
6. C	6. O	6. V	6. JJ
7. N	7. G	7. W	7. G
8. E	8. AA	8. X	8. P
9. J	9. A	9. I	9. Q
10. D	10. T	10. D	10. O
11. W	11. W	11. GG	11. I
12. T	12. L	12. M	12. II
13. O	13. D	13. Q	13. DD
14. F	14. K	14. F	14. AA
15. P	15. R	15. G	15. C
16. U	16. M	16. EE	16. V
17. K	17. J	17. L	17. X
18. B	18. BB	18. P	18. EE
19. S	19. B	19. B	19. J
20. G	20. N	20. CC	20. KK
21. L	21. C	21. J	21. PP
22. Q	22. H	22. DD	22. FF
23. I	23. S	23. E	23. M
	24. Y	24. A	24. Y
	25. F	25. S	25. OO
	26. Q	26. BB	26. LL
	27. E	27. R	27. E
	28. U	28. Z	28. H
		29. FF	29. N
		30. T	30. U
		31. O	31. Z
		32. C	32. F
		33. H	33. R
			34. HH
			35. D
			36. BB
			37. MM
			38. W
			39. S
			40. L
			41. B
			42. GG

ANSWERS TO CALIFORNIA'S EARLY CULTURES MAPPING

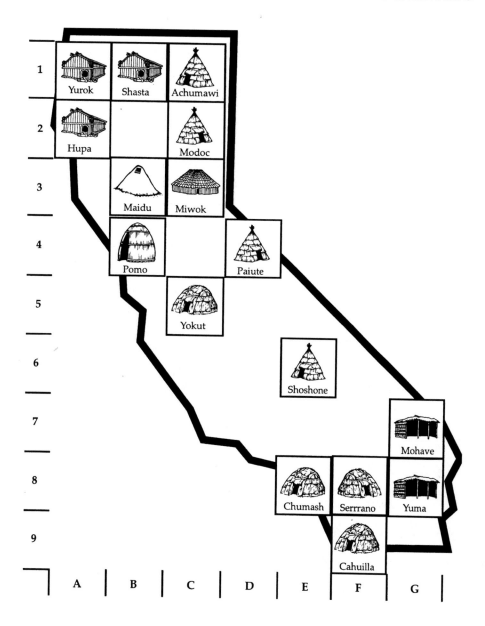

ANSWERS TO CONSIDER THE SOURCE

1. S
2. P
3. P
4. P
5. P
6. S
7. S

ANSWERS TO TIME TRAVEL

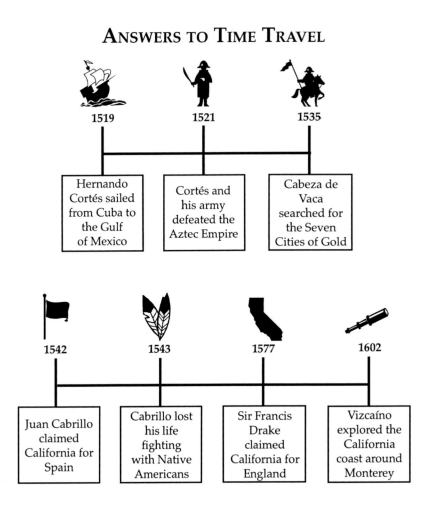

1519 — Hernando Cortés sailed from Cuba to the Gulf of Mexico

1521 — Cortés and his army defeated the Aztec Empire

1535 — Cabeza de Vaca searched for the Seven Cities of Gold

1542 — Juan Cabrillo claimed California for Spain

1543 — Cabrillo lost his life fighting with Native Americans

1577 — Sir Francis Drake claimed California for England

1602 — Vizcaíno explored the California coast around Monterey

MOUNTAIN MAN STORY GRADING CHART

CRITERIA	POINTS POSSIBLE	POINTS EARNED
Answering all Questions: Who were you?, What did you look like?, etc.	**50** Answered the 5 prewriting questions, 10 points each	
Spelling/Grammar	**20**	
Neatness of Final Draft	**15**	
Orally Reading Story	**15**	
TOTAL	**100**	

Answers to California's Missions Mapping Part I

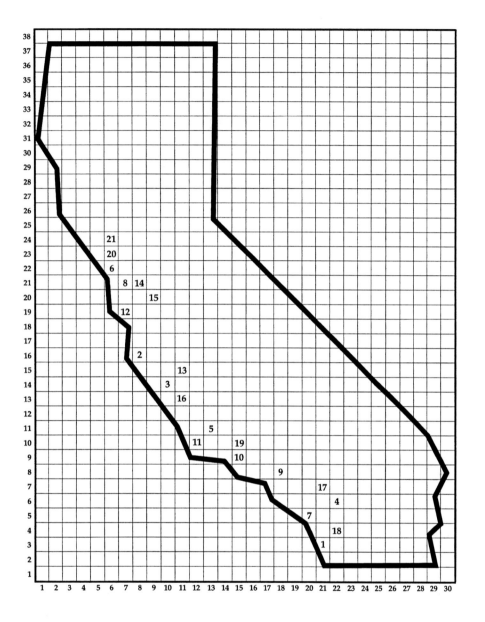

Answers to California's Missions Mapping Part II

1. California's missions were all built in western or southern California along the Pacific Coast.
2. Answers will vary, but should include information about the missions being built closely to the Pacific Ocean.
3. Answers will vary, but should include information about the missions being built closely together for protection, ease of travel, ease of control, etc.
4. Answers will vary.

Mexican War Grading Chart

CRITERIA	POINTS POSSIBLE	POINTS EARNED
Neatness	10	
Contains at least 2 facts about Mexican War	20	
Descriptions of Events	30	
Development of Character	30	
Orally Reading Letter	10	
TOTAL	**100**	

Writing Mechanics Rubric

CRITERIA	POINTS POSSIBLE	POINTS EARNED
Spelling	12	
Punctuation	12	
Grammar	12	
Capitalization	12	
Sentence Structure	12	
Heading	5	
Greeting	5	
Body (indent)	5	
Closing	5	
Signature	5	
Addressing Envelope	15	
TOTAL	**100**	

SANTA FE TRAIL JOURNAL GRADING CHART

CRITERIA	POINTS POSSIBLE	POINTS EARNED
Neatness	15	
Dated in Chronological Order	25	
Descriptions of Events	60	
TOTAL	**100**	

WRITING MECHANICS RUBRIC

CRITERIA	POINTS POSSIBLE	POINTS EARNED
Spelling	20	
Punctuation	20	
Grammar	20	
Capitalization	20	
Sentence Structure	20	
TOTAL	**100**	

GRID MATH ANSWERS

BIBLIOGRAPHY

Alter, Judy. (1998). *Santa Fe Trail.* Children's Press, New York.

Bois, Danuta: 'Bridget "Biddy" Mason' 1998 [Online] Available
<http://www.distinguishedwomen.com/biographies/mason-b.html>
(April 16, 2013)

Burgan, Michael. (2003). *It's My State: California.* Benchmark Books, Tarrytown, New York.

California. (2008). *Academic American Encyclopedia.*

California. (2008). *Collier's Encyclopedia.*

California. (2008). *Encyclopedia Americana.*

California. (2008). *Grolier's Encyclopedia.*

California. (2008). *World Book Encyclopedia.*

California History Collection: 'Early California History: An Overview' 2004 [Online] Available
<http://memory.loc.gov/ammem/cbhtml/cbintro.html> (April 16, 2013)

Families First: 'Historic Trails of the Old West' 1997 [Online] Available
<http://www.ida.net/users/lamar/trails.html> (April 16, 2013)

Headley, Amy and Smith, Victoria. (2003). *Do American History!* Splash! Publications, Glendale, Arizona

Headley, Amy and Smith, Victoria. (2003). *Do Arizona!* Splash! Publications, Glendale, Arizona.

Headley, Amy and Smith, Victoria. (2005). *Do California!* Splash! Publications, Glendale, Arizona.

Headley, Amy and Smith, Victoria. (2004). *Do Colorado!* Splash! Publications, Glendale, Arizona.

Headley, Amy and Smith, Victoria. (2004). *Do New Mexico!* Splash! Publications, Glendale, Arizona.

Hendricks, Ann. (1998). *America the Beautiful: California.* Children's Press, Danbury, Connecticut.

Kennedy, Teresa. (2001). *From Sea to Shining Sea: California.* Children's Press, Danbury, Connecticut.

Lexico Publishing Group: 'Dictionary.com' 2008 [Online] Available
<http://dictionary.reference.com/> (April 16, 2013)

Parker, Janice. (2001). *A Kid's Guide to American States: California.* Weigl Publishers, Inc. Mankato, Minnesota.

Pelta, Kathy. (2002). *Hello USA: California.* Lerner Publications, Minneapolis, Minnesota.

San Diego Historical Society: 'San Diego Biographies: Juan Rodriguez Cabrillo' 2001 [Online] Available <http://www.sandiegohistory.org/bio/cabrillo/cabrillo.htm> (April 16, 2013)

Santa Barbara Museum of Natural History: 'Chumash Life' 2004 [Online] Available <http://www.sbnature.org/research/anthro/chumash/intro.htm> (April 16, 2013)

Spartacus Educational: 'John Bidwell' 2004 [Online] Available <http://www.spartacus.schoolnet.co.uk/WWbidwell.htm> (February 4, 2009)

SunStar Media: 'Sea Otter Information' 1997 [Online] Available <<http://www.seaotters.org> (April 16, 2013)

University of Calgary: 'The Conquest of the Aztec Empire' 1997 [Online] Available <http://www.ucalgary.ca/applied_history/tutor/eurvoya/aztec.html> (April 16, 2013)

Woods, Mario. (1997). *The World of Native Americans.* Peter Bedrick Books, New York.